Teaching Yoga

How to Start, Run, and Grow Your Own Yoga Business

By: Discover Press

Table of Contents

Introduction

Dear reader,

This book intends to provide aspiring yoga teachers with a compass for this fulfilling yet onerous career path. I have felt the call to teach yoga after my practice bore its fruits, and I had begun turning to my mat to find harmony and peace. Through the practice, I found a space where I could be myself without judgment and begin healing my deepest wounds. Equally bountiful was the journey to find my voice as a teacher and learn how to trust my intuition. Witnessing the transformations and new powers gained by students through their yoga practice has become a main source of inspiration. My mission is to inspire students to create more space in the mind and body to live life more consciously.

It takes time and practice to learn the art of teaching yoga. No text can substitute the role of a mentor for guidance and inspiration. However, a book can contain useful information to aid in the path when you feel offshore and need to navigate the myriad of information available out there.

I organized this book following my personal experience. In part one, I explain the transition that occurs when we decide to embark on a journey to become teachers. In part two, I discuss the actual art of teaching yoga and the different tricks I've learned along the way. In part three, I talk about yoga in terms of finances, building a business, and how to create a sustainable and ethical career. The last part is an interview with yoga teacher Dorinda Farver. We talk about the struggles and joys of this profession and her experience as a successful studio owner.

Before delving into the book, let me introduce myself by sharing how I got here.

A Restless Youth

As a teen, I spent most of my days feeling disoriented, anxious, unable to relax, and always on edge. In hindsight, I realize unleashed emotions, and a lack of capacity to be present and focused, blindly led my behaviors. I was living in everlasting fighting mode.

Expressing emotions freely and openly is part of human nature. However, somewhere along the way, I began to restrain emotions and bury them deep inside the body, especially those deemed "negative." I had no model for how to healthily process feelings. Anger was fought with anger, fear was mocked, and shame was unacknowledged. My parents did not teach me how to deal with difficult emotions, as they also struggled with them. When those emotions showed up, I frequently felt embarrassed to talk about them, so I learned to repress them. However, my body's storage space for stuck energy and emotions is limited, and sometimes, my anger burst out of control. By the age of seventeen, unprocessed emotional energy reached the cap, and started overflowing into my physical body. I spiraled into depression and anxiety vortexes, and developed severe acne and amenorrhea. I did not halt until I broke completely and touched the ground.

At that time, my mum was renting a room to one of her colleagues, Silvia. She was the most put-together woman I knew, and I loved spending time around her unique energy. She was a yoga student going through her teacher training program, and one day, she invited me to attend a yoga class with her. I still wonder, if I didn't go, what would my life be like now? Yoga came at the right time for me to spring-start my transformation. I fell in love with the bliss that came post-class. I knew that not that all my anxieties would disappear, nor would all my wounds close, but I could resize them. Acne and

8

amenorrhea were not taking all my attention anymore. There was so much more out there.

For many years, yoga only occupied two hours of my life each week, but it slowly became a constant theme. My mat became witness to the most courageous choices I've ever made.

London – The Swinging City

Eventually, I decided to leave everything behind: my friends, my family, my hometown Bologna, my childhood nest, and the college I had just started—all to move to London. For the first time, both of my parents agreed that I was crazy and on the edge of ruining my life—typical Italian drama. I also started doubting myself, but I knew that I wanted to heal deep down in my heart, and going away was the right choice. In the Swinging City, away from my troubles back home, it was a period of hedonism and carelessness. Everything smelled unfamiliar and exotic, and I began to blossom. I was lost, and I found myself again, crying and laughing in the arms of new friends, made in a language I had just begun learning. There is a magic in being in a place where no one speaks your language: body language becomes a means to communicate. You learn to follow your intuition when you don't understand the verbal language. You read the information in the moment's energy and act consequently or experience a silence that can teach you more than a thousand words.

During my time in the city, I worked as an au pair for a South African-English family. In between dropping the child off at school and walking the dog, I filled my days by attending yoga classes at the nearby gym. I was always amazed and intimidated by the energy that emanated from yoga teachers: scary but mesmerizing. I bought my first mat and kept attending every class on the schedule until the mat began wearing down on the top and the bottom. I was slowly feeling one with my body for the first time in many years and for the first time in my adult life. There was not a particular day or moment that transformed me. The consistency of the practice started getting me out of the cyclical narrative and gave me the power to change my story—breaking out of my bonds. I wanted to learn more and more about yoga, and I started devouring all the classic and modern yoga texts. I read *The Bhagavad-Gita* for the first time (without understanding much of it) and *The Yoga Sūtra of Patañjali: Light on Life*, by B. K. S. Iyengar, *Siddhartha* by Hermann Hesse, and anything else that came into my hands.

The Netherlands: Sangha – Community

After about two years in London, I decided to enroll in college again, and I said goodbye once again. For the following three years, I studied at the local university in Breda, in the south of the Netherlands. While getting acquainted with the Dutch culture through riding my bike, smoking pot, and eating stroopwafels, a community was growing in the student dorm on the sticky floor of Easy Street. Through a newborn common passion for Acro yoga, every Saturday at 10:00 a.m., we had an appointment to play, learn new acrobatic skills, and share delicious food. The dynamics of an Acro yoga community are complex: in learning the skills, you also discover a new form of nonverbal trust and communication. We were opening the Saturday sessions with yoga and bonding exercises to warm up the group, then we were practicing Acro-skills and finishing with a Thai massage session. At first, I began leading different activities without much of a plan, just bringing in poses and exercises that I had learned through the years of yoga practice. I slowly started to improve and expand my skills related to partner yoga, massage, and group dynamics while attending Acro yoga workshops around the country. We were then coming back home with new tricks in the bag to teach. It was with this group that I discovered my passion for teaching yoga.

I always look back at that time in Breda with a smile. It was here that I began a more profound spiritual journey. I started experimenting with my diet, celibacy, and I got the first glimpse of the power of meditation.

Maastricht: The most productive year of my life.
After a few months after graduation, I moved again because I found a job in the city of Maastricht, only a few hours away from Breda. The following year was the busiest and most productive of my entire life. While working a 9-to-5 job and commuting, I began and finished my 200-hour yoga teacher training while climbing three times per week and practicing yoga the other two days. My Ashtanga practice, which I had begun back in Breda, gave me the enthusiasm and vigor to sustain those rhythms. I started teaching yoga at a squatting building and, after, I received my certification at a local yoga studio. I owe the start of my career to my wise and generous lead teachers, Dorinda and Robert, and the community at Yogasite in Breda.

At night, I taught and invested time and energy in my personal growth with activities that made me feel connected and alive. During the day, I was sitting at a desk, wearing a pretty dress, with a gray sky above my head, dreaming for the night to come when I could finally change out of my heels and into climbing shoes and leggings.

The line dividing my two worlds became thinner as the year passed by, until one day: June 2017. While drifting in and out during a yoga nidra session, I remembered something important. I remembered that I always wanted to leave and travel the world, but I had forgotten. My brain chemistry changed that day, and I just knew I had to pursue my crazy dream. In the weeks following the yoga nidra session, I started planning my exit. This was not the first time I'd decided to leave everything behind. When I moved to London, I arranged my departure in one week. It was a very rash decision, and it seemingly needed to be that way. This time, I wanted to take things slower, take care of everything, and leave without a trace. I had to empty and leave my apartment, all the things I had collected over four years; tell my friends, family, and colleagues; say goodbye to my students; and book a one-way plane ticket.

On my birthday, I organized a party with all the friends I met during my four years in the Netherlands, and I gave them most of my possessions. "Celebrate me by helping me feel lighter!" It was such a wonderful party, full of love, pizza, live music, and tears of joy and happiness. I planned to downsize and move out of my apartment by the end of September and rent a room for a few months to keep working and saving money. I did manage to move out of my house according to plan, but I didn't stay longer. A few days after my party, where I told all my friends about my upcoming new life adventure, my dear friend Elisah sent me a job ad for a yoga teacher and climbing guide in Vietnam. Although I hardly believed it was a real job, I applied anyway. One month later, I was on a plane to Hanoi in disbelief and unaware of all the beauty awaiting me on the other side. I spent my time between Mai Châu and Cát Bà Island, teaching yoga in old limestone caves and sharing my passion for the outdoors with colleagues that became friends.

Vietnam – Freedom!
My experience in Vietnam was briefer than expected. There were many reasons behind my choice, but only five months later, thirsty for new adventures and walls to climb, I left for Tonsai, a climbing gem nestled in between karsts in the south of Thailand. On the rough floors of the local yoga studio, again, I found a community of people that inspired, motivated, and taught new skills to each other. There was an abundance of energy, knowledge, and success to keep us going forever. I climbed, fell in love, taught yoga, jammed, and met my future husband while eating watermelon pancakes—not a good combo, trust me.

When our Thai visas were running out, we booked a flight to India, a place we had both longed to visit for a long time. Gregory David Roberts, the author of *Shantaram*, describes India in a way that that stuck with me, *"Indians are the Italians of Asia and vice versa. Every man in both countries is a singer when he is happy, and every woman is a dancer when she walks to the shop at the corner. For them, food is the music inside the body and music is the food inside the heart. The language of India and the language of Italy, they make every man a poet, and make something beautiful from every banalite. They are nations where love—amore, pyaar—makes a cavalier of a Borsalino on a street corner, and makes a princess of a peasant girl, if only for the second that her eyes meet yours."*

India – My journey within India.

You don't know exactly why you love her. She's dirty, poor, and infected; sometimes, she's a thief and a liar, often stinky, corrupt, miserable, and indifferent. But her spirit is boundless, and once you visit India, you can't do without it anymore. The experience that changed me the most was a ten-day meditation course called Vipassana. After completing it, it took me a long time to digest the experience into something that I understand today. Equanimity is an exercise in non-reactivity, of keeping calm despite harsh conditions. It is about not letting physical discomfort or a wandering mind define the moment-to-moment experience. Everything is constantly changing. Good times follow difficult times, which follow good times again.

When I entered the ten-day Vipassana meditation retreat, I searched for a better way to cope with stress and be more content with my life. There I found what I was looking for and much more. I still get angry, scared, ashamed, and still react to my emotions, but the extent to which I do is notably lessened. Most importantly, the realization that I have more self-discipline and inner strength than I ever realized has become a source of incredible optimism that empowers me to this day. Vipassana also enhanced my yoga practice; it almost gave it a new meaning or purpose. My Yin students often hear me saying that all the yoga I've done up to my first Vipassana was to prepare my back and hips to endure sitting meditations of eleven hours!

While visiting the birthplace of yoga, my practice started mutating. I became more and more inclined to meditate, and I began viewing poses as a tool to quiet my mind in its busiest moments. I began drifting away from the harsh discipline of Ashtanga to listen more to what my body needed on any given day: some days strength and some days kindness.

United States – The waiting room.

Two years later, I moved to the United States to unite with my travel partner, Tyler. In a heartbeat, I was on a new continent where I didn't have the right to work, enroll in a study program, or open a bank account. Legally, all I could do was wait. I became a master of waiting. Waiting for the immigration office to give me their approval to resume my life, I found myself at the mercy of the waiting room.

During that year, I sank into depression. I felt stuck on a Ferris wheel. One day I was on top of the world; the next, I was at rock bottom, over and over all year long. I desperately sought a purpose, something to fill my days because I had to convince myself that I didn't move to the other side of the world for love only. My perceived lack of worth made me feel empty and meaningless. During those days, the room felt dark, cold, and lonely. Other days I woke up, and my perception of the waiting room was completely different. I was aware of the impermanent nature of the situation that one day I would step outside and into a far more enticing stage in life. The embodiment of this knowledge allowed me to enjoy these groundless moments fully. I felt gratitude toward the freedom I had to explore my passions and enjoy my unproductive hobbies, giving bright colors to my life.

New Mexico – The discovery of Yin yoga.

Once again, my yoga and Vipassana practice were the tools I used to address my emotional instability. During this rough year, I discovered the practice of Yin yoga and its intrinsic connection with meditation and the Vipassana wisdom. Along with everything that I get passionate about, I began learning and practicing Yin and took several specialization courses. Yin was the complementary part of my practice and teaching.

Due to my work condition and my mental instability, I took a sabbatical year from teaching. I began again during the pandemic, when people needed yoga the most, and when I felt ready to start again. I had no network in the United States yet, so I first organized classes for my friends and family online. Then someone contacted me on LinkedIn, and I got a gig teaching at a virtual studio where I continue teaching today. When things opened up again, I found a yoga studio here in the city of Albuquerque. In just three months, I was once again teaching ten classes a week.

I couldn't survive on the salary I was making teaching yoga, yet I couldn't teach more classes. I had to find an alternative income. I was drawn to the digital marketing field through a direct demand from needing to advertise my classes. I crafted my content, learned how to edit videos, and marketed to get people to join my classes. Through helping other teachers with their online presence, I realized that I liked digital marketing. It's fun, it triggers my creativity, and I don't have to move my body. When Covid-19 hit, I enrolled in a digital marketing boot camp at the University of Denver, which helped me whet my skills and learn new ones. I got certified with the highest grade and was invited to be a teacher assistant for an upcoming course. Nowadays, I teach only the number of classes my body can handle, and I get the other part of my income through freelancing projects while sitting comfortably at a desk.

It took me five years to feel confident as a yoga teacher. Not that I was a bad teacher, or my classes lacked worth, but I had to master my craft and sharpen my voice. I also had to learn where to draw the line between compromising the respect I have for this ancient wisdom of India and making a living in this industry. Yoga is a lifelong discipline, and my teaching style and personal practice will keep evolving along the way. Your students and the journey of teaching yoga will take you out of your comfort zone and into places you will never have imagined visiting. Take this guide with you and enjoy the ride.

I truly wish you all the best,

Andrea

From A to Z: The Art and Business of Teaching Yoga

Part I – From Student to Teacher

Yoga has been a devotional practice free of charge for centuries; a sacred wisdom passed on from master to student. I will kick off this book by introducing the circumstances in which the current wellness industry emerged, starting with a brief history of yoga. On the one hand, it gives me the chance to provide you with a historical context of why we can make a living doing what we love and why there is an economic opportunity for it. On the other hand, I am a true advocate of helping any aspiring teachers become aware of the threats that the commercialization of yoga is bringing to this ancient wisdom and the people of India.

In the following chapters of Part I, I will talk about transitioning from being a yoga student to wanting to be a teacher. Afterward, I get into the details about the most popular routes to becoming a yoga teacher and give you an overview of the different training programs available. If you only retain one thing from this chapter, be sure it is the metrics on choosing a valuable teacher training that is worth your time and money.

A Brief History of Yoga

The evolution of yoga can be traced back to over 5,000 years ago. Some historians think it may be up to 10,000 years old. Early thoughts on yoga were transcribed on palm leaves that were easily damaged, destroyed, or lost. Most teachings were transmitted orally. Therefore, we cannot be certain about its origin.

Yoga's transformation is long, rich, and very complicated. Its history is a jumble of various ideas, beliefs, and techniques that often contrast with one another. A systematic account of the events and thoughts that shaped yoga as we perceive it today does not exist because its history is more like a tree rather than a straight line. However, to make this complex subject more approachable, I comply with a traditional timeline. For brevity, the history of yoga is divided into four main periods: **Pre-Classical Yoga**, **Classical Yoga**, **Post-Classical Yoga**, and **Modern Yoga**.

It is beyond the scope of this book to talk about history. However, it is vital to know the context in which the modern wellness movement worth more than $84 billion worldwide was born.

Pre-Classical Yoga: 2500BCE–1100CE

The word yoga was first mentioned in the oldest sacred texts, the Rig Veda, derived from the Sanskrit root "Yuj," which means to join or unite. Composed by the Indus-Sarasvati civilization in Northern India, the Vedas were a collection of texts containing songs and mantras used by Brahmans, the Vedic priests, during their rituals and prayers. The Upanishads were written over a period ranging from 700 to 400 BCE and originated from each branch of Vedas.

The word Upanishad comes from the roots "upa" (near) and "shad" (to sit). It comes from the idea of sitting near the feet of the teacher. Upanishads are texts on spiritual knowledge and philosophy written as support to the Vedas. The most renowned of the Upanishads is the Bhagavad- Gita, composed around 500 BCE.

In the Vedas, yoga is not described as a path to liberation, and asana practice is not described at all. Rather, yoga, among its many other meanings, meant discipline, and the closest word to asana was "asundi," which described a block upon which one sat, supposedly to meditate.

Vedic priests were generally self-disciplined and avoided any forms of indulgence; they performed sacrifices known as yajna, and used poses that most researchers believe are the precursor of the kind of yoga poses we use today.

Classical Yoga: 200BCE–1100CE

The wisdom of the *Yoga-Sûtras* characterizes the Classical period. The Sutras were written by a man named Patanjali, but when they were composed is not certain. The alleged author lived somewhere between the second and fourth century BC and was presumably Indian. Patanjali is a figure shrouded in mystery about whom many stories are told—one of those narrates that he fell from heaven in the form of a snake to bring yoga to humanity.

The Yoga-Sûtras are the first known systematic approach to yoga. It is a collection of aphorisms that offer guidelines to live a meaningful and purposeful life. It is important to mention that it is not a book meant to be read and studied as we do with text nowadays, but instead was embodied with the guidance of an experienced teacher.

According to the philosophy of this period, humanity suffers because of the illusion of separation between the individual consciousness and universal consciousness. The physical senses were seen as a distraction to the final liberation. The Yoga-Sûtras offered a clear path for how to achieve enlightenment and embrace that union again.

Patanjali introduced the physical practice of yoga to prepare the student for the deeper practices of meditation. However, besides being listed as one of the eight limbs of yoga, asana is only mentioned in three of the 196 Sûtras.

Patanjali is often considered the father of yoga, and his Yoga-Sûtras have strongly influenced most modern yoga schools.

Post-Classical Yoga: 700CE–1800CE

A few centuries after Patanjali brought out the Sûtras, yoga masters began straying from this classical philosophy to create a system of practices designed to rejuvenate the body and prolong life. Thus, it is the beginning of Tantra yoga, not to be confused with modern Neo-Tantrism. With revolutionary techniques to cleanse and restore the body and mind, Tantra yoga moved away from the path of austerity and sense of withdrawal described in the Sûtras to embrace the physical body as a gift. Exploring these physical-spiritual connections with body-centered practices led to creating what we primarily think of yoga in the West: Hatha yoga.

One of the oldest existing documents we have describing Hatha yoga is the *Hatha Yoga Pradipika*, written between the 14th and 15th centuries CE by Svātmārāma. This text is almost twice as long as the *Yoga-Sûtras*. Compared to today's traditional yoga, it too has minimal asana practices described. Instead, it extensively covers the practice of pranayama and the mudras. In the section discussing asanas, only fifteen are explained, and of these, most are done while sitting on the floor. As time went on, later texts expanded the number of asanas explained. For example, the *Gheranda Samhita*, written around the late 1600s, describes thirty-two poses. A few decades later, the *Shiva Samhita* listed eighty-four asanas.

Modern Period: 1800CE to Today

During the British Raj, the rule by the British Crown on the Indian subcontinent from 1858 to 1947, wrestling, gymnastics, martial arts, and other exercises began cross-fertilizing the asana practice. This gradual evolution moved the yoga practice away from the fundamental idea of holding seated poses for a long time as a preparation for meditation, toward a more active yang style of building strength and health that characterized the wellness movement in the '90s in the U.S. and Europe. As a result, the Sanskrit term "Hatha" became an umbrella term for all physical postures of yoga. In the West, Hatha yoga refers to all the styles of yoga (Ashtanga, Iyengar, etc.) that are grounded in a physical practice.

In the late 1800s and early 1900s, yoga masters began to travel to the West, attracting attention and followers. Yoga first came to the U.S. in 1893, at an interfaith conference held at the World's Parliament of Religions in Chicago when Swami Vivekananda (12 January 1863 – 4 July 1902) impressed the attendees with his lectures. The yoga that Vivekananda presented to American audiences was different than the versions most are familiar with today. He spoke about yoga as a matter of philosophy, psychology, and self-improvement. His published lectures are flooded with the word "power," and in one of them, he urges his listeners to "Stand as a rock; you are indestructible." Vivekananda's approach to yoga did not include the flowing sequences of asanas or postures that we learn as practice at a studio. When Vivekananda spoke and wrote to

Americans about yoga, he described it as a type of diet, a method of concentrating the mind, and pranayamas, breathing techniques. He enriched his lectures with fantastic stories of Indian wonders and groups of stage magicians who wore turbans and robes for their routines; these tales contributed to the initial Western perception of yoga as magical. Many Americans assumed that yogis held supernatural powers.

The renaissance of the posture-based forms of yoga happened in the early 20th century, as Mark Singleton explains in his 2010 book, *Yoga Body*, when Indian traditions of Hatha or physical yoga merged with Western forms of physical culture. One of the most relevant figures was Swami Vivekananda, who helped set the stage for yoga's modern iterations. While Swami Vivekananda has often mocked Hatha yoga to his American audiences—calling it "gymnastics"—he taught a few postures to a small crowd in New York City.

According to Suzanne Newcombe, author of *Yoga in Britain*, Vivekananda "marks a turning point in how Indian religiosity was understood outside of India." Moreover, Vivekananda's story inspired several other Indian teachers to follow his example and come to the United States over the next few decades. Among them was Yogananda, the founder of the Self-Realization Fellowship and author of *Autobiography of a Yogi*.

In the 1920s and '30s in India, Tirumalai Krishnamacharya strongly promoted Hatha yoga, Swami Sivananda, and other yogis practicing Hatha yoga. In 1924, Krishnamacharya opened the first Hatha yoga school in Mysore. Ten years later, Swami Sivananda Saraswati founded the Divine Life Society, one of the most well-known Hindu spiritual organizations and an ashram, founded in 1936, in Rishikesh, India. Four students of Krishnamacharya went on to be major influencers in Western yoga and would continue his legacy and increase the popularity of Hatha yoga: B.K.S. Iyengar, T.K.V. Desikachar, Pattabhi Jois, and Indra Devi. The importation of yoga to the West continued at a trickle until Indra Devi opened her yoga studio in Hollywood in 1947.

The Modern Yoga Industry

Within thirty years, yoga became an industry worth more than $84 billion worldwide, according to the 2016 Yoga in America Study.

The 2016 Yoga in America Study is a national study conducted by Yoga Journal and Yoga Alliance that benchmarked similar studies carried out in 2008 and 2012 by Yoga Journal.

For this study, Yoga Journal and Yoga Alliance partnered with Ipsos Public Affairs to expand the understanding of yoga practice in America and determine how Americans view yoga. This study confirmed that the Wellness Movement is already booming and is only expected to grow.

Yoga is gaining popularity - The number of yoga practitioners in the U.S. has increased to over 36 million in 2016, up from 20.4 million in 2012. In addition, 28% of all Americans have participated in a yoga class at some point in their lives.

Yoga is slowly becoming more inclusive - More male and older practitioners than ever before started to practice yoga (approximately 10 million male practitioners and almost 14 million practitioners over the age of 50—up from about 4 million men and 4 million 55+ year-olds in 2012). Nevertheless, it is still a very white-predominant practice. There is still a lot of work to do to spread yoga among all U.S. communities and make it overall inclusive. We will talk more about inclusivity later on in this chapter and in the following one about how to learn to teach yoga.

Yoga boosts the economy - Practitioners report spending over $16 billion on clothing, equipment, classes, and accessories in 2016, up from $10 billion in 2012.

Yoga is trendy - Thirty-four percent of Americans say they are somewhat or very likely to practice yoga in the next twelve months—equal to more than 80 million Americans. Reasons cited include flexibility, stress relief, and fitness.

People practice for multiple reasons - The top five reasons for starting yoga are flexibility (61%), stress relief (56%), general fitness (49%), improve overall health (49%), and physical fitness (44%).

The success of this industry gives us as teachers and studio owners the opportunity to earn a living doing what we love.

The Second Colonization of India

I am aware that I am an imperfect messenger of the role the U.S. plays in the cultural appropriation of religious and sacred components of India's identity. The yoga world is abundant with middle-class white women with big ideas about what other people should do. I own Lululemon pants, and I teach at a hot yoga studio. I am guilty, too. I always do my best to make choices that do not disregard this ancient wisdom, and I encourage students and future teachers to do the same. I choose to speak my mind on this sensitive subject to not further perpetuate the issue.

Cultural appropriation is the adoption of an element of one culture by members of another culture. Adopting the fashion, iconography, trends, or styles from another culture is a form of cultural appropriation. We live and consume elements belonging to other cultures assimilated into our own every day, often without realizing it. When members of a dominant culture appropriate from minority identities, it becomes controversial.

I want to take a moment to reflect and understand how intimately linked the history of yoga practice in the United States and Europe is with centuries of colonization and oppression. Most of us are not aware that yoga and Ayurveda were banned in India under British Raj, and the practices millions of Westerners now turn to for alternative medicine were once mocked and prohibited.

Since its first introduction at the World's Parliament of Religions in Chicago, yoga has evolved more in the last sixty years than in its entire history. Many esteemed and highly spiritual teachers from Eastern and Western traditions have contributed to its diversification and spread of the practice to a European and American audience. To meet the Western needs of fitting everything into scientific maps, experts carried out several studies of the spiritual and physical bodies, which inevitably increased its popularity among the masses and boosted the industry.

Eastern elements have been banned from studios or commercialized on yoga apparel. These days, anything goes with the word: Goat Yoga, Beer Yoga, Hot Yoga, Harry Potter Yoga. I've heard people say that the more people practice yoga in any shape or form, the more the world will benefit. It is not my intention to judge anyone's path. Still, it's also essential to recognize that yoga has been around for thousands of years and is a devotional practice free from cost that is now being marketed and sold as a commodity. As practitioners and teachers, it's our role to acknowledge where this industry is heading and shield yoga as a devotional practice from undergoing a second colonization. This colonization is the misrepresentation of yoga's true origin.

Mastery of the body through the practice of asanas is what most of the Western world perceives as yoga. Yoga was and still is a *spiritual* practice. It has always been a physical practice for its own sake, but it will never be purely that for the true yoga practitioner. Nor is it a practice purely aimed at "stress-reduction" to function better in a capitalist society. Yoga is much more than asana. It's a process. It's active awareness. It's the way you engage with the world to create harmony. Yoga is how we participate and create relationships. Asana is a tool at our disposal to remove blockages and have a healthy body.

When someone completes a yoga teacher training that is primarily asana-based and remains completely unaware of the complexity of the roots of the practices, they are culturally appropriating yoga. By remaining ignorant of the history and complexity from which yoga springs and the challenges it has faced under Western culture, they perpetuate a recolonization of it by stripping its essence away.

There can be authentic cultural appreciation through cultural exchange, harmony, and understanding. In one of its many meanings, yoga means liberation from every shape and form, including that of race, gender, time, space, location, identity, and even history itself.

However, a multi-billion-dollar industry now makes a profit by taking yoga out of its original context to rebrand it and repackage it for monetary gain. Teachers and students are responsible for addressing this, or else we perpetuate its second colonization, where we might eventually eradicate the true essence of the practice.

According to Rina Deshpande's opinion, most yoga purchasers are oblivious to what they are consuming. And that is what we need to change together, by asking deeper questions such as:
- "Do I understand the history of the yoga practice I'm so freely allowed to practice today, though it was once ridiculed and prohibited by colonists in India?"

- "As I continue to learn, am I comfortable with the practices and purchases I'm choosing to make, or should I make some changes?"
- "Does the practice I live promote peace and integrity for all?"

Educating ourselves, like the practice of yoga itself, is slow but steady progress. Start where you are—from asana or philosophy, you may have already developed a lot of awareness that is becoming more finely tuned.

Becoming a Yoga Teacher: Are You Ready to Embrace This Journey?

Teaching yoga is immensely rewarding and challenging at the same time. You have the space to provide students with the tools they need to grow physically, mentally, emotionally, and spiritually. Witnessing your students begin that journey is one of the most gratifying aspects of being a yoga teacher. However, it is also a challenging profession. Being a good yoga teacher implies embodying yoga outside the class as well. The role you will cover comes with many responsibilities. It does not mean that you need to be perfect or showcase an ideal image of yourself, but you will notice that if you do not do what you preach in class, you will not sound as natural, and your message will be less penetrating.

To become a certified yoga teacher, you should first complete a teacher training program. I'm using the verb should on purpose here because it is not mandatory, though many studios require you to have completed one. You will learn why later on in the chapter.

Often there are no prerequisites to enroll in a TT program (teacher training program), so everyone can de facto become a yoga teacher.

Enrolling in a TT program does not imply that you want to teach. Some people do it to deepen their knowledge of yoga, or because they feel stuck in their practice, or to find a community of like-minded people. There are so many wonderful reasons to enroll in a TT program. Although this book addresses people that intend to teach, this chapter can be helpful to anyone thinking about enrolling in a TT program.

Does a 200-hour certificate allow you to teach yoga? In most places, it's required. Does a certificate make you a good yoga teacher? No.

Yoga had inevitably followed an evolutionary process, and if it weren't for its physicality and "post-yoga-bliss" feelings, it would likely not have become so popular in the West. Yoga brings together physical and mental disciplines to achieve liberation. Traditional yoga philosophy requires that students adhere to this mission through behavior, diet, and meditation.

However, to accommodate the wishes of Western practitioners, many studios and TT programs have abandoned the mental discipline side and promoted only the asana practice. That is often what interests most students. Many prospective teachers miss that yoga is a lifelong process of balanced living and is a mind-body type of complementary and alternative medicine practice. It requires many years of training and, with teacher training programs that last for only a month, only a smattering of information is given regarding the other limbs of yoga.

Many students, including myself, have started practicing asana because it feels good. Only years later, I started investigating why yoga made me feel good on a mental level. Asana introduced me to two things that are immensely important in meditation: the power of the breath to connect the mind to the present moment and how to tune in wholly to the sensations in the body, both gross and minute. The physical practice was the gateway preparation for seated meditation. It was when I understood this connection that I decided to become a yoga teacher. The changes in the behavior and the diet followed naturally, without being imposed or forced by myself or my teachers.

Be humble. There are indeed no requirements to participate in a TT program, whether or not you mean to teach afterward. My advice to fully benefit from a TT program is to have been practicing for a few years with the same teacher, have an established practice, and have noticed improvements in your life outside the mat before embarking on this journey.

With that said, the following chapters will give you a better understanding of how to become a yoga teacher, what programs are available, who regulates those programs, and how to choose the best one for you.

EveryBODY Can Teach

I have been so lucky to have had the guidance of highly spiritual teachers over the years: some were Indians, some were Westerners, one was African. Some were old, some younger, some women—but the majority were men. A few were overweight; some were very athletic. All of them, though, existed in yoga. Everything I remember from their teachings was not the poses they taught me— they often were simple ones—but how they spoke to my soul and me. They provided a safe space in the class where I was allowed to be vulnerable. They heard me. And they all contributed to my transformation. Yoga changed my life, and I will be forever grateful to my teachers.

I also had very competent teachers at "doing" yoga, but did not leave me with any new mindfulness knowledge, nor were their classes a welcoming space to turn inward. Often their classes transformed into great sweaty workouts with loud music, but nothing more.

I have never thought about inclusivity because I and the baggage I was carrying within me have always felt welcome, included, and visible in yoga studios. Not having to think about inclusivity is a privilege. I find others in these spaces who look like me, have stories similar to my own, and use language similar to mine.

Every type of body can practice and teach yoga. A lot of students wanting to be teachers have Instagram and social media influencers as role models. They think that they need to perform all the poses or name them in Sanskrit to start teaching. Turning into a pretzel will not make you a teacher. Though, it might make you a good gymnast.

Due to the emphasis on asana practice in the West, we often estimate teachers based on their fitness level rather than the energy they radiate or the pureness of their heart.

Many marginalized people, whether LGBTQ, overweight or underweight, BIPOC, disabled, or other, or, more than likely, some combination of these and other identities, often do not feel welcomed by the environments formulated in "modern" yoga studios. The settings and the language used are not inclusive, and they do not offer space for every type of body to grow.

"If you feel isolated in class because you do not see yourself reflected in your studio, you are not alone! Do not try to fit into the culture of the studio; move on to find your own tribe." - Sangha

Yoga means to include us all because everyone has a soul. Everyone can grow through yoga, and everyone can support other's growth on the mat, even if they will never practice inversions or only practice three poses. The best teachers speak through their souls, not purely through their bodies. They feel the vibe of the class, what they truly need—not what their ego wants. And they make it happen, even when they are not following the protocol of the studio (of course, always keeping students safe and respecting boundaries).

Now that we have covered reasons for becoming a yoga teacher with good and bad examples, I will attempt to demystify yoga teacher training programs. In the following chapters, I discuss the history of TT programs; how, when, and why these programs were born; who regulates them, and why it is such a challenging mission. In the last part, you will get some tips on choosing a TT program that is right for you among the hundreds that are out there.

Teacher Training Programs

Understanding 200-, 300-, and 500-hour RYT Programs

Since there is a lot of information circulating out there, becoming a yoga teacher is a topic that most students find confusing. I will provide some clarity.

Several types of yoga teacher training (YTT) programs are available, and some are more widely recognized and often required if you want to teach at a studio.

For the sake of simplicity, we will focus on Registered Yoga School (RYS) and Registered Yoga Training (RYT), which are registered trademarks of the Yoga Alliance. The two primary designations awarded are RYS 200 and RYS 500. The differences have to do with the number of hours of training. There are two ways to earn a 500-hour certification. The first is to attend an RYS-500 school and complete all of the training there. The second is by completing a 200-hour followed by another 300-hour training.

Once you complete the training, you receive a teaching certificate that makes you a Certified Yoga Teacher (CYT). You can then submit your certificate to the Yoga Alliance for verification, pay an annual fee, and become a Registered Yoga Teacher (RYT 200 or RYT 500). We will talk more about Yoga Alliance later on.

200-hour Yoga Teacher Training

In June 2019, Yoga Alliance launched new Elevated Standards—a core curriculum and competency for Registered Yoga Schools to follow through the program. The curriculum outlines only 75% of the 200-hour training, so schools and teachers still have some room to personalize it. The YA did not give guidelines regarding the prerequisites students need to meet to enroll in the program, so it is entirely up to the school to make their choices.

During the program, you will learn the fundamentals of:
- Techniques, training, and practice 75-hour: asana, pranayama, and meditation
- Rudiments of anatomy and physiology 30-hour
- Yoga humanities 30-hour: history, philosophy, ethics
- Professional essential 30-hour: teaching methodology, professional development, practicum

500-hour Yoga Teacher Training

For the 500-hour and 300-hour programs, the Yoga Alliance does not provide such an in-depth curriculum yet. It is in the making and will be released in 2021. However, schools still need to have their curriculum approved to allow students to become RYT 500. Generally, a 500-hour program has additional units added to the 200-hour curriculum and goes deeper into the different aspects of yoga, allowing for more time to develop skills for teaching. The requirements to enroll in a 500-hour program are the same as the ones for a 200-hour program.

An RYS 500 training will incorporate training hours in the following educational categories:

- **Techniques, Training, and Practice:** 150 hours – Topics in this category could include, but are not limited to: asanas, pranayamas, kriyas, chanting, mantra, meditation, and other traditional yoga techniques. These hours must be a mix of analytical training in teaching and practicing the techniques and guided practice of the techniques themselves.

- **Teaching Methodology:** 30 hours – Communication skills such as group dynamics, time management, and the establishment of priorities and boundaries; how to address the specific needs of individuals and special populations, to the degree possible in a group setting; principles of demonstration, observation, assisting and correcting; teaching styles; qualities of a teacher; the student learning process; business aspects of teaching yoga (including marketing and legal).
- **Anatomy and Physiology:** 35 hours – Includes both the study of anatomy and physiology and its application to yoga practice. A minimum of fifteen hours is spent applying anatomy and physiology principles to yoga.
- **Yoga Philosophy, Lifestyle, and Ethics for Yoga Teachers:** 60 hours – Topics in this category could include, but are not limited to: the study of yoga philosophies and traditional texts (such as the Yoga Sûtras, Hatha Yoga Pradipika, or Bhagavad-Gita); yoga lifestyle, such as the precept of non-violence (ahimsa), and the concepts of dharma and karma; ethics for yoga teachers, such as those involving teacher-student relationships and community and understanding the value of teaching yoga as a service to others (seva).
- **Practicum:** 40 hours – Topics in this category include: practice teaching as the lead instructor; receiving and giving feedback; observing others teaching; assisting students while someone else is teaching.
- The remaining 245 contact hours are distributed amongst the educational categories based on the school training's focus.

A 300-hour yoga teacher certification is the next level of education for yoga teachers who have completed their 200-hour yoga instructor training, which is the minimum requirement. To register for advanced training, you may be expected to have a minimum number of teaching hours under your belt. Every program has a different emphasis on a particular limb or branch of yoga.

To register your 500-hour certificate on Yoga Alliance and become RYT 500, you need to follow the procedure for the 200-hour. Additionally, you are required to register a minimum of 500 hours as a lead instructor in a classroom.

Other Types of Yoga Related Training

The training programs mentioned above are the most common ones but are also not the only options available.

Whether or not you have completed your initial 200-hour, many programs branch out from the more standard ones and can go more in-depth with a specific type of yoga. Specialized training courses can take the form of 50-hour, 100-hour, or even 200-hour courses. They can be alternatives to the traditional 300-hour advanced yoga teacher training, or they can allow you to pursue a topic of your interest without having to invest a large amount of money. The following is not an exhaustive list of courses you can choose from.

Specialized Training Courses for Teachers (who have already completed 200-hour)

The length of these programs varies between 20 to 100 hours. They often require students to have completed a 200-hour program already.

Yin Yoga Teacher Training	Yin yoga has a very different philosophy than traditional Yang practices and focuses on entirely different functions in the body; it is often treated as specialized training.
Yoga Nidra Teacher Training	Yoga nidra is a completely guided meditation practice. It aims to restore the physical and mental well-being through the therapeutic powers of active rest.
Kids' Yoga Teacher Training	Kids' yoga is one area which most 200-hour teacher training programs do not encapsulate in their core curriculum. Children's yoga classes are very different from the average adult asana class. Therefore, kids' yoga teacher training is invaluable if you want to teach yoga to a younger audience. You will learn the appropriate goals for next-generation yogis at each developmental stage, how to structure children's yoga classes, and significant teaching methodologies for captivating children's attention and guiding them to a more aware, meditative state. If you plan to teach yoga to kids, my

	suggestion is to enroll in a YA-recognized program.
Hatha Yoga Teacher Training	Often Hatha yoga is an umbrella term to describe different types of yoga. Nowadays, most Yoga Teacher Training programs teach a hybrid between more classical Hatha yoga and modern Vinyasa. The difference between these two styles lay in the pace of the practice: while Vinyasa is most likely a flow where poses are choreographically connected, in a Hatha class, you can expect a more well-rounded practice,

	and you tend to hold poses for a longer time.
Tantra Yoga Teacher Training	Far from the sexualized version of the Neo-Tantra, Tantra is an ancient path to yogic union. Tantra is about channeling the energy naturally present in the body-mind system to reach a higher state of being. Asanas, pranayama meditation, chanting, and mantras are the main tools used by traditional tantric teachers and central in teacher training.

Ashtanga Yoga Teacher Training	An Ashtanga asana practice is marked by a universal sequence of yoga postures known as a "series." If you aspire to become formally certified in Ashtanga yoga, you must study with the founder's grandson, Sharath Jois, in Mysore, India. At present, only he can "authorize" a yoga teacher to share Ashtanga yoga with others. However, there are other yoga teacher training programs led by advanced Ashtangis that can give you an equally good introduction to the practice.
Iyengar Yoga Teacher Training	Iyengar yoga is differentiated from other methods by a world-wide, standardized system of instruction. Certified Iyengar Yoga Teachers (CIYTs) undergo rigorous training and evaluation to earn their certifications. Candidates must study for a minimum of three years with a recognized teacher, complete a 500-hour training or equivalent program, complete an apprenticeship, and pass two levels of intense testing and evaluation.

Kundalini Teacher Training	KRI (Kundalini Research Institute) is the official international training organization that promotes the teachings of Yogi Bhajan and oversees Kundalini teacher training programs. The Level One KRI Aquarian Teacher Training Program consists of a 220-hour program (180 hours in class; 40 hours of home practice). Graduates of Level One earn the title of KRI Certified Instructor of Kundalini Yoga as taught by Yogi Bhajan®, are registered with the International Kundalini Yoga Teachers Association (IKYTA), and fulfill the Yoga Alliance RYT (Registered Yoga Teacher) 200-hour requirement. The primary regulatory body for Kundalini Yoga teachers is IKYTA, not Yoga Alliance.

Forrest Yoga Teacher Training	The Forrest Yoga Foundation Teacher Training is a 27-day immersion that encompasses 22 days of intensives and teacher training, 3 days of anatomy, and a 10-hour Forrest Yoga Business Course. This teacher training is the first step to becoming certified as a Forrest Yoga Teacher. All Forrest Yoga Teacher Trainings are Yoga Alliance approved.
Bikram Yoga Teacher Training	Bikram Yoga is a sequence of 26 yoga postures practiced in a heated studio, known as the Bikram Yoga sequence. Students must train with Bikram Choudhury, the creator of Bikram yoga in Los Angeles, to become official Bikram teachers. You must have at least six months of experience practicing Bikram at an official studio or equivalent home practice to be admitted. You must also provide a letter of recommendation from your Bikram instructor. The minimum age for a Bikram instructor is 21 years old. The cost for training is $11,400, which includes

	accommodations during the training. The Bikram sequence is not patented and the Yoga Alliance does not recognize the training.

This is not an exhaustive list of specialized courses; for the sake of brevity, I focused on the ones I am the most familiar with. Depending on which specialization you are interested in, there is likely something out there for you. Not described above: Trauma-Informed Yoga Teacher Training, Meditation Teacher Training, and Yoga for Cancer (Y4C) Teacher Training.

Certification of Individual Yoga Therapists

Everything mentioned previously falls into the category of "yoga teaching." However, another ramification is essential to touch upon, which is known as "yoga therapy."

A yoga therapist applies yoga techniques to specific health conditions. Therefore, they must train in both the methods (asana, pranayama, chanting, philosophy or point of view, and meditation) and the therapeutic applications of these techniques.

A yoga therapist must also know the conditions they are working with and, during their studies, are trained to look at health conditions through a yoga therapy lens and assess from a Western medicine perspective.

Yoga therapy is the process of empowering individuals to progress toward improved health and well-being by applying the teachings and practices of yoga.

Although yoga teachers and yoga therapists are usually lifelong learners, the training entry point for yoga therapists is much higher. The IAYT (International Association of Yoga Therapists) has set standards with a minimum training time of 800 hours, in addition to the prerequisite of a 200-hour yoga teacher training. Also, yoga therapy schools are tasked with graduating competent yoga therapists with a proven ability to work with medical conditions safely and effectively.

Since yoga therapists are always yoga teachers, it is easy to see why the public can get easily confused. Yoga therapists often play both roles—teaching interested students yoga and working individually with clients with health challenges.

Most essential is that those with physical or mental health issues looking to yoga for help consult with a yoga therapist instead of a yoga teacher.

Individualized education from a yoga therapist will have much better outcomes and minimize the chance of an untrained yoga teacher inflicting harm due to a lack of knowledge and education.

How Much Does a Yoga Teacher Training Cost?

The cost of yoga certification can vary greatly depending on the type of training, the location, the yoga teacher, the yoga school, and whether it is immersive and all-inclusive or spread out. The price can fall anywhere from $200 to $7,000. For example, a 200-hour yoga teacher training will generally run from $1,000 to $3,000, and a more advanced yoga certification course typically ranges from $1,000 to $7,000.

Here is a breakdown of the price range and duration for yoga teacher training courses:

Type of TTC	Price Range	Duration
Specializations	$200 – $999	1 week – 3 weeks
200 Hour TTC	$999 – $4,000	3 weeks – 4 weeks
300 Hour TTC	$1,000 – $7,000	3 weeks – 5 weeks
500 Hour TTC	$1,500 – $15,000	3 weeks – 8 weeks

The Difference Between Intensive or Spread Out Trainings

If you have a timeline of when you want to have your teacher training completed or a certain amount of time you can take off from work, this chapter will help narrow down your choices.

The majority of schools choose to lay out the 200-hour or 300-hour training in two main ways:

- **Intensive** – This training takes place all at once, with days back-to-back and usually lasts for a month. Generally speaking, you can expect to start your days early in the morning and finish in the evening; all the training hours must be completed within that short time frame. As these days are done consecutively, you may have to consider if your commitments will allow you to step away for that time and if this teaching method is the best for you.

- **Spread out** – Some programs break out the 200- or 300-hour during evenings and/or weekends. Each school might have a different schedule to address its demographics. These programs take longer than a month to complete, and they work best for those who cannot set aside large blocks of time. Some schools might also include a full intensive week at the end of their training.

Which one should I choose?

Although you will walk away with the same diploma, each layout offers a very different experience.

Intensive programs are exactly that—intense. These types of training are designed to immerse yourself into the practice of yoga fully. Some intensives are held within a city; they might or might not offer food and/or accommodations or be all-inclusive. City environments can give you the chance to maintain some connections to work, friends, and family and at the same time be more budget-friendly. Going abroad will take you away from your day-to-day life's distractions and help you go deeper into your studies. Intensive programs held aboard are all inclusive and pricier.

Spread-out training programs are best for those who cannot step away from their commitments for a prolonged period. They cover the material over several months. Each layout can be different; some programs are held only during the weekends to accommodate Monday through Friday obligations, and some are held one or two evenings a week.

For example, my TT program was spread out into an entire weekend each month, sometimes including Friday. It took me a year to complete the 200-hour, but I was in no rush. I enjoyed having a full month to digest the practice and information received during the weekend.

Some programs are broken down into two or more longer periods, for example, two weeks at a time. In this way, a student can get the experience of both formats without needing to take one large chunk of time off.

There is no "best" format, only what works best for you—asking other teachers about their personal experiences is the best way to shed light.

The Role of Regulating Bodies in Teaching Yoga

To become a yoga teacher, you need to start teaching yoga. There are no shortcuts. As of 2021, there is still not an official governing body overseeing the yoga teaching world. However, many organizations have been trying to take on the difficult task of regulating teacher training programs on a national, international, and even global level. For the sake of brevity, I assume that my primary audience is Americans. Hence, I bring attention to the most predominant U.S.-based registries. Before talking about Yoga Alliance and Yoga Unify, let's look at teacher training programs' accounts.

The history behind teacher training programs

Before the early 1990s, there were hardly any yoga studios in the U.S. Yoga culture then was like surfing culture today: people learned from others, practiced independently, and occasionally met in groups to practice. With the birth of the modern fitness culture, yoga classes began to mold themselves after dance classes. The modern "yoga class" was born, and people left their living room to join their local studios.

Before the fitness boom, yoga in the U.S. was practiced primarily by hippies and people interested in Hinduism and Buddhism. Their yoga was gentle and focused on meditation. Yoga would not have benefited from the fitness explosion had it not been for the Ashtanga yoga from K. Pattabhi Jois, which led to creating the Vinyasa style. These styles of yoga are sweaty and get one's heartbeat high, similar to that of aerobic classes. These classes soon became very popular among fitness enthusiasts and triggered the start of the yoga industry.

Before the rise of teacher training programs in the 1990s, yoga teachers qualified by showing up regularly at classes. Eventually, they'd be asked to substitute for the instructor, and soon, they started their own teaching journey.

When yoga exploded in the 1990s and studios started popping up at every corner of Los Angeles and San Francisco, there were not enough teachers to accommodate the high demand. There was no time to develop teachers the old-fashioned way, so teacher training programs began to "mass-produce" teachers to meet the new market demand.

A global need of regulating yoga teaching

Gradually, a fear emerged in the community that the quality of yoga offered would widely vary without regulating yoga teaching. This includes the general safety of the practice, as well. The response around the world to this problem was to set up organizations that could regulate and oversee the global standards of yoga teaching.

In 1987, several national yoga governing bodies, mainly European and South American, joined forces to establish the International Yoga Federation to set worldwide yoga standards. With headquarters in France and Uruguay, the International Yoga Federation is still the largest yoga governing body in the world.

At the same time and for the same reasons, many senior yogis felt the urge to set national standards for training yoga teachers in the U.S. In May 1997, at a Yoga Journal conference, discussions began to establish a non-profit organization to do just that. Two years later, the Yoga Alliance was founded.

Yoga Alliance

Founded in the U.S. in 1999, Yoga Alliance is the second-largest nonprofit association representing the yoga community—with over 7,000 Registered Yoga Schools (RYS) and more than 100,000 Registered Yoga Teachers (RYT) from all over the world, as of April 2020. Their mission is to "foster and support the high quality, safe, accessible, and equitable teaching of yoga."

To become a Registered Yoga Teacher, you need to have completed a minimum of a 200-hour program at a certified school.

The difficult role of the Yoga Alliance: The difference between qualified and certified teachers.

To bring consistency to the yoga world, the Yoga Alliance established minimum standards for teacher training programs. Teaching programs that fulfill those requirements can become a Registered Yoga School (RYS). Graduates of these schools can then apply to be registered on the Yoga Alliance Registry as a Registered Yoga Teacher (RYT). Yoga Alliance does not provide any teacher training courses or certifications. It is purely a listing of teachers and schools that meet their minimum requirements.

When you complete a yoga teacher training course, you are a "qualified" yoga teacher. However, due to the lack of official yoga certification, the yoga community has formed itself into alliances and wheels to ensure that the teaching of yoga remains within high-quality standards. As a result, those looking to do teacher training can choose courses of a high standard as judged by the curriculum, faculty, and lead teacher.

An RYT certificate does not automatically mean that you are knowledgeable, that you are reliable, or that you are trustworthy. The Yoga Alliance has been accused of being just an expensive marketing tool many times. There is still plenty of work to do to shrink the gap and ensure that a YA certification for both teachers and schools means quality yoga and respect for old traditions.

There are many schools of thought on whether it's good to become a Yoga Alliance certified yoga teacher. Some within the yoga world feel that most students will rarely know or care whether you are registered with any governing bodies. It is not free to become a member, and not all the certified schools comply with the Yoga Alliance's standards.

On the other hand, the yoga world is growing rapidly, and without some way of keeping a check on the standards of teaching yoga, the reputation and good name of yoga itself may well be in danger of being tarnished. Becoming a member has its benefits: its size and reputation, and having your details on the YA listings can attract new students to your classes or training courses. They also offer discounts on insurance and yoga equipment, opportunities to network with other teachers and studio owners, and information on training courses and workshops.

It wasn't until late 2020 that I decided to join the Yoga Alliance and become a registered teacher. At the rate the yoga industry is growing, particularly in the U.S., it is necessary to have a national body that regulates it to preserve its integrity. I believe in the good intentions behind the Yoga Alliance's work, despite their stumbles, and that's why they have my trust.

Yoga Unify

Yoga Unify (YŪ) is a nonprofit organization that launched in September 2020. Heather Shereé Titus, the co-founder of YŪ, says that it intends to set new standards for yoga teachers, prioritize ethics, provide educational resources to students, and unify the community in ways that Yoga Alliance (YA) has not.

From the YŪ website: "Our goal is not to standardize, but to create healthy and sustainable standards within which individuals can truly thrive—the individual lineages, schools, teachers, and students that make yoga the beautifully diverse and universally powerful practice it was meant to be. There's a lot to be done, but the power is in our capable hands."

Titus announces that YŪ will be a governing body that represents the yoga community thoroughly.

"If every student who begins a serious practice of yoga is guided to become a teacher, then we naturally have an imbalance," explains Titus in an interview published in the Yoga Journal. "Unfortunately, it's become common practice for yoga studios to mass-produce teacher training programs for survival. The issue is only intensified by the proliferation of teacher training programs offered online during COVID." According to Heather, it resulted in an over-saturation of teachers, many of whom graduate with the bare-minimum qualifications and have little class experience.

"This is why we support the lifelong student journey as something to be honored on its own merits." YŪ aims at offerings courses at various levels for different styles and specialties that outline a clear education plan—similar to the 100-, 200-, and 300-level trainings we are familiar with.

"We see yoga as a field of study and practice, rather than a commercial industry, and we seek to move yoga in that direction," Titus says. "We don't buy into the idea that 'X' number of hours makes a yoga teacher."

Yoga Unify plans to certify yoga teachers and schools through continuous evaluation and peer review, recognizing their level of professional experience and specialization in a public directory. The YŪ governing council is in charge of deciding these credentials. Whenever a teacher desires to further her education, Yoga Unify advisors suggest that a teacher chooses a specific study pathway to prepare them for advancement. YŪ recognizes yoga teacher certifications and reassesses teachers based on new standards that evaluate a teacher's experience and expertise.

The YŪ directory highlights credentials and experience and allows teachers to upload videos, articles, and other promotional and educational material. In this way, students can search for the type of class, training, or mentorship they are looking for.

Choosing a Teaching Training

You have decided to begin a new venture and enroll in yoga teacher training. It is an exciting and life-changing experience that you are about to embark on. Your first teacher training represents not only the foundation from which you will learn the rudiments on how to teach, but it will also provide you with a "sangha"—a community that will support your personal and professional growth, which in yoga are unified. The studio offering the program might also become the springboard to your new career. Courses to become teachers are often an investment and unfortunately, there are many out there that offer poor education. It is crucial to make wise choices, and this chapter will provide you with a framework that will help you make the right choice for you.

Set your intention
First of all, to narrow down choices and reach your goals, it is essential to know what you hope to get out of your program. For example, some students know they want to become teachers; some want to deepen their practice and discover later that they want to teach yoga. If you want to learn a particular style or lineage, find training specializing in that. Most 200-hour programs will teach various yoga styles, but as explained earlier you can find specially focused ones.

If you are not interested in teaching yoga but only looking to deepen your practice, look for a yoga school that focuses more on the topics you are genuinely interested in. Sometimes a teacher training might not be the best option, but a specialization course is what you are looking for.

If you aim at teaching yoga, look for a studio or school that follows a teaching methodology that you can see yourself using. If teaching at a specific yoga studio calls you, I highly recommend doing your training there. Some studios have a unique teaching style and require their teachers to do an in-house training. Consider asking your favorite teacher where they did their training.

Answering these questions will help you find the right program and the right lead teacher for you.

The teachers

The lead teacher is one of the most fundamental aspects of a growth-oriented program. If you resonate with a particular teacher, ask them directly or research online if they run a TT program. If you do not have a favorite teacher, before committing to any teacher training, ensure that the program has qualified teachers that you feel comfortable with and investigate the lead teachers involved.

Requirements to enroll in the program

Looking at the teacher training requirements is a great benchmark to make sure they run on high standards. A lot of schools still have stringent requirements for students to attend their teacher training. If a program is selective with its attendees, you can assume that they consider yoga a lifetime practice; they take their job to train future teachers seriously. However, don't be too strict about it. I did my teacher training at a school with no requirements (or bare minimum), and I would still highly recommend it.

Duration

Do you have the time available required by the program? The duration of the program is something you need to take into account long before committing to it to avoid unpleasant surprises. As we extensively covered in the different outlines of teacher training, courses can last for several months or run as an immersion style. Some take place on weekends.

Outside the course duration, you should anticipate time for study, assignments, and practice teaching. Ensure practice time is included, where students teach each other, or the opportunity to teach an actual class is provided. Studying yoga is essential for your growth, whether reading or writing assignments, as this broadens your studies and allows you to explore beyond class time.

A yoga teacher's training should not be stressful but a pleasure to attend. If you don't have enough time now because you already have too much on your plate, you can work out a plan for the future.

Cost

Take this advice: do not go with the cheapest option. That piece of paper at the end of the program is worthless if you learned nothing. Courses are expensive, some studios or teachers charge more than they should, but many others will charge a fair rate. Typically expect to pay something between $999–$5000 for 200-hour training (non-inclusive). If you do the math, when a program costs $5000, you are technically paying $25 per hour, which in my opinion, is a fair price for high-quality education. Many schools offer different payment methods or even scholarships. If you do not have enough money now for the teacher training of your dreams, it is worth waiting a little longer rather than enrolling in the cheapest option.

200-hour vs 500-hour yoga teacher training

Many students, myself included, have wondered whether to enroll directly in a 500-hour program. But, after talking with few teachers, I opted out of it.

A high-quality 200-hour program was an excellent starting point and provided me with a solid foundation. However, I was already teaching in a non-studio setting, and I wanted to verify whether teaching yoga was my vocation.

As with any profession, creating a vibrant teaching practice that combines knowledge and wisdom requires more study. Therefore, I decided to spread out the training by beginning to teach after the 200-hour training and then continue the education after feeling more established in my role as a teacher.

200-hour online teacher training

Becoming a good yoga teacher takes time. It is a life-long practice. Wasting money with short programs or instant certifications without much work is not wise, particularly if this is your first 200-hour program. Use this time to deepen your practice instead. We have lived through a pandemic, and remote is the only option available, but in my humble opinion, it is worth waiting until it is safe to practice together again.

Only when you work with a hands-on teacher over a long time, can you expect results. The energy that teachers bring to the class is irreplaceable. Asking questions and interacting with fellow students also is a fundamental part of live teaching programs. Online students tend to miss out on the community that is created in a hands-on course.

Most importantly, it is harder to learn teaching nuances from an online option. It is perfectly acceptable for programs to outline part of their courses online. Technology allows flexibility for students and teachers.

However, online short specialization programs, like 20-, 50-, and 100-hour programs, are good for already experienced teachers.

Cultivate a Beginner's Mind: You Are Always a Student

Good teachers become great teachers when they improve their skills and expand their knowledge through continuing education.

Therefore, with the risk of sounding repetitive, yoga is a lifelong practice.

Your first 200-hour training brings you into the field, where you get a glimpse of many techniques and styles, but only on a superficial level. It is only through continuing education, under the tutelage of trusted teachers, that you can dive deeper into a limb of yoga and master it. CE challenges you to outgrow old frameworks and press on to new levels of comprehension.

Further education allows teachers to keep the "beginner's mind" active and to stay curious. Many great teachers must hold space for physical, emotional, spiritual, and intellectual evolution. They take time off each year so they can revisit what it is like to be a student. This attitude can help them relate to students in a more effective way; it gives them time to turn into "receiver" instead of "giver."

Most licensed vocations (including physical therapy, psychology, and the like) require that people complete continuing education to maintain licensure. The emergence of this requirement is an active area of development in our nascent yet growing community. Yoga Alliance requires RYTs to complete yoga-related training to maintain their registration.

Pursuing further knowledge is a non-negotiable aspect of being a credible, ethical, professional yoga teacher.

Part II – Learning the Art of Teaching Yoga

Your yoga teacher training has created a platform for your transformation, as well as the people you hope to teach. Along with learning the rudiments of teaching yoga, you have nurtured your practice, which is paramount to finding your authentic voice as a yoga teacher. It takes commitment, courage, and vulnerability to step over the barriers to knowing your true self and grow authentically. There are no shortcuts to self-knowledge, only time and patience.

We tend to find comfort in the ideas of who we think we are or who we think we should be as yoga teachers instead of leaning into the process. However, this is not what you want to hear when you're making your way across the awkwardness and overwhelming feelings of being a new teacher. It is now time to learn your craft.

Learn Your Craft

It is impossible to focus on understanding yourself if you are also trying to figure out how to teach yoga. If you are learning how to drive a vehicle, you need to know how to operate the car before playing with the audio system. It takes time to become fluent in a skill, but the only way to create the bandwidth for self-study is to be grounded and comfortable in your craft. Start devoting yourself to your studies, practice teaching yoga, and be patient.

Everyone had to start somewhere; even the most experienced teacher you know was terrified when she taught her first yoga class. She had to learn how to transfer her wisdom and knowledge of yoga into words for the students and how to understand the needs of the class and make sure everyone felt safe and welcome. The responsibilities that the role of a teacher carries are extensive; this topic deserves a much deeper discussion than what I intend to offer here.

Hearing the accounts of others as they grappled with finding their authenticity will surely help you along your journey. In the following chapters, I look over the experiences I went through when I was learning to teach and find my authenticity in class, the struggles I faced along the way, and what tools were useful, hoping that you can learn from my successes.

I have been teaching yoga for a little over five years now. I teach in English, my non-native language, as I am also writing this book. When I was a rookie, several teachers told me it was their intuition to guide them in a class, so I waited. And waited. But no one else came to teach my class, not even my intuition. There was no magic involved, but there were years of discomfort and cold feet before finding my true voice as a teacher.

I planned classes, practiced instructions, and drew stick figures to visualize the sequence better. I was also borrowing—I borrowed so much from other teachers, and I am thankful for all the feedback I have received from them. When I started teaching, the difference from when I started teaching is that now I do not always stick to the plan, but I do let my intuition guide me. I have masted this skill enough that I am comfortable improvising from the plan.

Later on, in part two, I talk about my first experiences teaching and the most likely places where you can start teaching yoga to the public.

Turning an Art into Science

I still remember my dismay and panic when I led my first yoga class at a studio. I constantly thought about the next pose and how to formulate cues to lead students into a transition. I thought about what words to use to keep people engaged, the beginning and the ending of the class, how to touch my students, and if my hands were too cold or too hot or too sweaty.

After I saw that half of the students had their right leg forward and the other half had their left one, I left the studio thinking that teaching was not my vocation. And here I am, five years later, still practicing and still teaching with joy and compassion, and still having half of the class facing me and half facing the opposite direction.

The anxiety of being in front of students waiting for me to give instructions did not wholly disappear. I am always scared I'll go blank and not think about the next pose for the rest of the class and witness all my students—one by one—roll their yoga mat and never look back. That is my deepest irrational fear as a yoga teacher.
I have learned to manage my stress by getting ready for every class and precisely knowing what pose follows the other. Then, if I blank, I can peek at my notes and remember what follows.

In the first year or two of my teaching career, I planned every detail for my classes, formulated cues, how to pronounce them, how many breath cycles for each pose, and what inclusive language to use. Then, at one point, I started teaching at a studio that urged teachers to use music. So, I started planning my playlists as well.

I memorize the sequences beforehand to be fully present for my students, so I don't need to think about the actual poses. I can pay attention to them. My energy is in the room, not in my head. I can then connect with my intuition and trust what I know, feel, see, and hear. Intuition is the ability to understand how to do something without thinking. Understanding that we all have intuition-power is essential, but it is not a skill taught at teacher training. It only comes with time and devotion to the practice.

This learning process was time-consuming but worth it. Now it takes me a fraction of the time to get ready for a class, and I have an arsenal of lessons at my disposal. Most importantly, I walk into a class more confident. So, here are my practical tools to help you along the way.

When You Start, Keep It Simple

My first suggestion is to keep your classes familiar and straightforward, particularly when you have just begun teaching. Create a comfort sequence and teach that to your students. Here is a revelation for you: hours of practice, patience, and repetition are required to improve and develop in yoga. If classes are too varied and a student learns a new pose constantly, steady progress will be absent.

I went to yoga classes held in an Ayurvedic medical studio in Pondicherry, India. I repeated the same flow every morning for two weeks straight. I'm not talking about Ashtanga's series, but an elementary Hatha class. Every day was equally beautiful. Students do not grasp all the cues at once. As a student, I noticed that the sequence was the same, but I never questioned it or thought that the teacher was too "lazy" to change it. Returning to the same poses every time helps students to change their viewpoints and focus their attention on a different layer of the practice.

I also repeat my Yin classes. I play with 10–15 poses and shift them around. After all, there are only 26 total Yin postures, variation included. Hatha or Yin, progression lies in mastering simplicity.

Repetition allows progress. It takes many moon cycles to master a yoga pose and experience its physical benefit. A yoga class is not designed to entertain students' minds but rather to help them progress in their practice.

Keep your classes, whatever style you teach, simple. Then, with experience, more complex sequences will flow more freely. Or maybe they never will, as in the case of my Indian teacher, and that is also fine.

Plan Your Class Around a Theme

Before I start to sketch a sequence of poses, I think about the central theme of the class. The theme represents the red thread for the class. For example, for a heart-opening themed class, I choose a flow that includes backbends and back strengthening poses; if the theme is patience, I let students hold poses for a longer time.

Sometimes, my theme is a pivotal pose, with I often choose for my power classes. For instance, if I select Eka Pada Galavasana—flying pigeon—as the central asana, before and after class, I draw attention to the parts of the body involved in its execution.

I do not always tell my students what the theme of the class is. If I do, I often choose a moment in the beginning.

In the past, I would research themes, often in yoga books. Now, I mainly let my intuition or events happening in my day guide me in the choice.

Music or No Music in Your Yoga Class?

I tend to avoid playing music in a yoga class. I find it distracting for myself and my students. Music tends to turn me outward rather than inward. I discourage you from hiding your voice behind a playlist, especially at the beginning. However, if music is essential for you:

- Avoid hip-hop, pop, and rap music.
- Try to use songs with no words, as students can get lost in their meanings.
- Craft your playlist in a way that flows with your flow.

Suppose the studio is surrounded by the noises of the city. In that case, music can be a tool to disconnect from that external world and turn the senses inward, as long as it does not entertain students and therefore create another form of distraction. Find music that does not dictate the pace and rhythm of the class.

The Time of the Day

The time of day you teach is an essential factor to consider when planning a class. Even when the style is already established, I usually serve morning classes with a more vigorous and warming practice. Therefore, I choose themes that invoke energy, while evening classes can lend themselves to slower flows and poses are held longer. In this case, my themes will often assist students in relaxing and preparing to sleep.

Demographics of the Class

It is crucial to teach those that show up in your class. If you have a room full of beginners, create a more beginner-friendly class. Think about the average student that attends your class, and then outline your sequence with that specific skill level in mind. Remember to be inclusive: it is better to teach a simple flow that beginners can follow, even if there are few more advanced students in class. You can add complexity by offering enriching elements to the postures you are instructing. This way, students of all levels will have an offering in your class.

The Groove of a Class

I craft my flows on my mat with pen and paper while rehearsing what I plan to let my students do in my upcoming class. I have a notebook designed for that purpose, and it comes with me to every class I teach. When my creative energy is low, I revisit old lessons and play around with sequences to turn them into something new; when my creative energy is high, I start from scratch. Other times, I draw inspiration from classes I attended from other teachers.

My flows have an intro, a verse, a pre-chorus, a chorus, a bridge, and an outro, just like a song.

Intro - Like the beginning of a film or novel, a class introduction should catch students' attention without overwhelming them. For this reason, openings are typically slower and more low-key. The goal is to bring the students to the present moment, let their day be washed away from the body, and get them curious about the practice to come.

Verse - The verse is a chance to be creative and explore the different sensations I am trying to bring out in my students. All the major muscle groups and joints start to be activated as far as their optimal range of motion comfortably allows.

Pre-chorus - Although optional, a pre-chorus helps to introduce the chorus. A pre-chorus usually contains a repetition. For instance, in a morning class, I tend to do a sun salutation; moon salutation in the evening. If the climax of the flow is a pose or a series of postures, I can introduce some of them more slowly to create familiarity with it.

Chorus - The chorus is the culmination of all the big ideas in the flow. It is a summary of the theme. It serves as the climax to the flow. Everything that came before had prepared the body for this moment.

Bridge - The bridge typically happens after the main pose, toward the end of the class. The point of the bridge is to remind students that there's more to this class and I suggest practicing counterposes or prolonged static holds.

Outro - Asanas performed in the outro should signal clearly to the body that the class is coming to an end. In other words, we are slowing down. Whatever style you are teaching, allow for extended cool-down periods at the end of every practice so that students can comfortably make their way through Shavasana.

The above-mentioned is not a strict template to follow but a good starting point to develop a class. One can, for example, work first with the right side of the body and then repeat everything on the other side. In this case, the pre-chorus, the chorus, and the bridge would repeat twice.

Time Management

In a yoga class, it is crucial to start and end on time, to respect the needs of everyone. You will learn how to manage time with experience, but at the beginning, it can frankly be quite hard, and you often rush to Shavasana or finish too early.

Depending on the structure and length of the class, you want to allocate the right amount of time for the beginning of the class (intro and verse), the middle (pre-chorus and chorus), and the ending (bridge and outro). Part of planning is to decide how much time I want to spend on a particular section. I use a watch to help me stay on track during class. If you are running out of time, it is better to skip a few poses than rush the ending.

Like in music, the intro and outro are equally important because they give space to students to assess their state before and after the practice.

Verbal Cueing

Although my yoga environment and teacher training were held in English, I did not have the mastery of the language to give instructions verbally.

Explaining to students how to get into a pose and the body parts to engage—least of all to name muscles and bones—was a new challenge I had to face if I wanted to keep teaching outside Italy.

Cues for a yoga pose do not just come out of your mouth through some magical channeling. Giving clear, compelling verbal cues is one of the most distinctive characteristics of a good teacher. Like all skills, I could significantly improve my verbal cues with a clear strategy and practice.

Learn from other teachers
I started attending yoga classes with a different ear. I was paying attention to how other teachers formulated their instructions and how much space was left between each cue. You can learn so much by just listening.

Use landmarks to describe directions
One of the most helpful tips I have learned by observing other teachers is to use landmarks. Beginners and more advanced students suddenly cannot distinguish right from left anymore, or which way is up and which way is down. Providing landmarks that describe which direction the student is moving, such as the wall, the door, the window, rather than just telling them to turn left or right, will help them orient in space and minimize this confusion. Even when

I teach online, I use the orientation of the mat and the screen as landmarks.

Learn students' names

Learning student's names is the easiest thing I can do and the best way to make my communication direct and relevant. In addition, personalizing instructions make teaching more skillful and intimate.

Plan and rehearse cues

There are poses that I teach almost in every class. I feel confident enough about my cues that I even dare with my words, which are enough to express myself without demonstrating the pose. Other asanas that I do not teach often or have difficult transitions from one pose to another, I plan the instructions and rehearse them at home while planning the class. I try to keep my cues as simple as possible with a language that everyone can understand. Not everyone knows what the serratus muscle is or how to engage it, and a yoga class is not an anatomy class. However, under the right circumstances, I spend time explaining the reason behind unfamiliar cues I give.

Some teachers, myself included, are tempted to fill every second of class with instruction, anticipation, knowledge, personal discovery, and more. Try not to overwhelm your students with too many instructions. Stick to an average of three instructions per pose and let them be with the discomfort of the silence. That is where most of the growth happens.

Feedback Is Essential for Growth

Other teachers and expert practitioners can give you valuable feedback for your maturity as a yoga instructor about your sequence, energy in class, verbal cueing, etc. It is normal to feel intimidated by the presence of another teacher in the room. Recognize that they are not there to judge you but are there to support your growth.

I discourage asking students for feedback regarding the way you teach; we will talk more about this in the role and responsibilities of the teacher later on in the chapter.

The Art of Emulating (without being a parrot)

As I have mentioned multiple times already, I tend to borrow from other teachers: expressions, themes, cues, sequences, and music. Therefore, taking and studying other teachers' classes enables me to improve constantly, even without a more experienced teacher nearby.

Cennino Cennini (born c. 1370) in his manual *Il Libro dell'arte* – "The book of art" written between 1396 and 1437, suggested as a means to skill-up by "constantly copying the best things which you can find done by the hand of great masters. And if you are in a place where many good masters have been, so much the better for you. But I give you this advice: take care to select the best one every time and the one who has the greatest reputation." When done right, copying leads to new development and growth; but it is more or less plagiarism if you blindly mimic it. I have learned a couple of tips to avoid pure imitation, and I will share them with you now.

Validate what you are borrowing. Sometimes other teachers say things that are not universally true, particularly regarding anatomy and alignments. So, before you repeat it back to your students, understand if the affirmation aligns with your experience and knowledge.

Use simple words. Rephrasing things in your own words will help you better understand what you are trying to communicate, and the delivery will stick better in your student's heart.

Rehearse. If you like a sequence, try it out and make sure you can cue it correctly before teaching it to your students.

Hands-On Adjustments

There is no book to learn about hands-on adjustment. The right place to do it is on your mat, with the help of an experienced teacher to guide you.

More teachers practice a hands-off approach to assist students, and more yogis wonder where the line is between helpful and inappropriate. I want to share my thinking on this touchy debate and offer advice to help keep everyone safe in class: you and your students.

As a student, I have experienced a lot of hands-on adjustments to my body. Very competent teachers have touched me, and their hands have helped deepen my knowledge of yoga and proprioception. Proprioception is one's awareness of the position and movement of the body.

However, this is my personal experience, and I avoid assuming that everyone else around me had the same.

Ask for consent. There is no such thing as implied consent in yoga or anywhere else, for that matter. The touch from a stranger can be traumatizing, and you do not know the personal history of your students. There are many ways to ask your audience whether it is okay for you to touch them. The most important thing is to use a language that empowers students to opt-in for hands-on assisting rather than opt-out. It creates an inclusive atmosphere and allows people who are comfortable with it to stand out, rather than requiring those who might already struggle to speak up, to make a move.

Know what needs adjusting. Your touch needs to be firm and gentle simultaneously; otherwise, the student might misinterpret the intention behind it. If you do not know exactly how to adjust a pose, stay away from it.

As a teacher, I always had mixed feelings about touching students. I used to be a massage therapist, and I practice Acro yoga and partner yoga. So for me, connecting body parts is a natural form of communication. I get to know people, and I heal through touch. However, not all yoga students are comfortable with getting a massage. And a yoga studio might not be the right place to explore this realm.

We live in an increasingly litigious society, and the #metoo movement has brought a heightened awareness to the power dynamics that too often had happened in yoga settings.

It is a natural human behavior to crave the affection of the person in charge, and it can lead to developing a distorted image of the role of a teacher in the student's mind. For me, this piece of information was a valid reason to be more reserved in interacting with my students. I usually do not make hands-on adjustments. I touch my students (with their consent) by applying pressure with my hands, for example, on their lower back in child's pose. Touch, when appropriate, can lead to the creation of a safe and welcoming environment where everyone feels supported in their growth.

I opted out of traditional hands-on adjustment because the majority of alignments we learn during teacher training not only do not make sense for me, but they can harm the body in the long term. Or better, they make sense to reach the aesthetic of a pose but do not strive for the body's optimal health. If you are interested in this topic, I highly recommend reading *Your Body, Your Yoga* by Bernie Clark. It was during his Yin yoga teacher training that I had a lightbulb moment. Each one of us is different. You would not drive a car with my glasses. So, why are there universal yoga alignments? Why does everyone have their knees face in the same direction or feet equally distant?

Rather than direct the attention to how a pose looks, teachers should instead focus on how a pose feels. "How does it feel?" is the right question to ask the student before intervening and making any adjustments. Then, if they feel good in the targeted areas of the pose, I let my student be.

However, this is my school of thought, and I still comply with a few traditional cues. When I want a student to be more engaged in an action, I try simply touching the area that needs attention. For example, in Warrior II, I tap the back arm to remind students to engage that muscle. Instead of a more dynamic adjustment where the teacher makes the action happen for the student, tapping or pointing in this way brings awareness to a muscle that may be sleepy.

Touching students drains energy. That is another reason why I often do not put my hands on my students. When my energies are low, or I feel sick or for any other reason, I preserve my powers by avoiding physical contact.

Dealing with Fatigue

Fatigue is a common problem for yoga teachers. It is easy to get carried away with always wanting to teach astonishing classes, and most of us are very passionate about our work—I am no different. Teaching yoga is not my full-time job because I realized that I could not teach more than ten hours per week; otherwise, I risk burnout.

At the studio, I teach many Vinyasa-based classes to beginners. Therefore, I tend to perform most of the sequence. I also move my body when I practice and prepare for my classes; and another passion of mine is rock climbing, so I train and climb outdoors every other weekend. If I do not take care of myself and give my body time to rest and recover, I get fatigued easily. When I am in this state, I do not find joy in teaching, and I drag my body everywhere. A general feeling of unhappiness takes over. Fortunately, I know what it takes to avoid fatigue.

I need to sleep a lot and wake up early in the morning. I do not have a good day if I am constantly tired and longing to nap. There are no short-cuts or magic pills to replace a long restorative night. Watching TV in the evening does not help my sleep. I do my best to avoid screen time during the week or to have people over.

My practice of yoga and meditation is even more critical when I teach seven hours per week. I have a lot of students asking about my yoga. It varies depending on the season, what style I am teaching, and my energy level. My practice has evolved a lot since I began yoga. For example, in spring, I favor a session of pranayama followed by meditation rather than asanas. But in winter, when I tend to feel lethargic, a good power class in the morning helps me set an energetic tone for the day.

There are no rules for your practice. However, taking care of your body and mind is a prerogative when you teach so many hours a week and juggle work, school, kids, partners, pets, and friends.

Good food makes me feel good. Eating healthy food helps energy levels. I make time to cook meals that make me feel satisfied. I do not need to create gourmet meals every day; I keep my food relatively simple, and I eat organic. I try to limit my sweet intake to once a week as a treat.

I listen to my body, and I am not scared of missing out. It all comes down to listening to our body, slowing down when we need to, and spending quality time with ourselves. It implies turning down invites, glasses of wine, movie nights, and sometimes climbing adventures with my partner. I cannot be a good role model for my students if I do not put my health first.

"The good (shreya) and the pleasant (preya) are two different things. They motivate a person to pursue two different goals. The one who embraces the good meets with auspiciousness. But the one who chooses the pleasant is lost."
— Katha Upanishad 1.2.1

With this verse, Yamaraja, the Lord of Death, begins to unravel the difference between short and long-term pleasure. The story of Nachiketa and Yamaraja explains that we are constantly faced with choosing one of two paths: preya, the lure of temporary enjoyment and ego satisfaction, or shreya, the commitment to do what is beneficial in the long run, which will help us attain the lasting, eternal fulfillment of self-realization.

Ethical Guidelines for a Yoga Teacher

Yoga is an integrated way of living based on moral standards—traditionally called "virtues" considered universal for humankind. Patanjali encoded part of these virtues in the first limb of its Yoga-Sûtra, called Yama ("discipline" or "restraint"). This category is composed of the following five virtues: non-harming (Ahimsâ), truthfulness (Satya), non-stealing (Asteya), chastity (Brahmacharya), and greedlessness (Aparigraha). Other key texts of yoga also include kindness, compassion, generosity, patience, helpfulness, forgiveness, purity, and so on. These are virtues connected to the "good" person.

All this wonderful yoga philosophy we have learned during yoga teacher training does not mean anything unless we practice it and make a difference in ourselves and our community. As teachers, we have a great responsibility toward our students, and our behavior inside the class needs to reflect the high moral standards advocated in yoga.

At the same time, we need to consider the present-day socio-cultural context, which differs in many ways from the conditions of pre-modern India. We are not medical professionals that can diagnose and treat injuries; we are not psychologists or physiotherapists. We are not even traditional spiritual guides, so what are we?

I found a simple yet clear definition of a yoga teacher's role: "to teach and guide students in the practice of yoga, motivating them to grow in their mind, body, and spirit by demonstrating poses, creating an intentional plan for each session, and setting an environment conducive to mindful, relaxing and focused class."

When teachers are "successful" at teaching yoga, students tend to idolize them and put them on a pedestal by dehumanizing the person and assuming that she does not undergo everyday challenges. This devotion from the students can lead to the teacher's ego creeping up and driving their choices. It is not abnormal for thriving, famous teachers to struggle with their ego, but any teacher willing to be vulnerable and honest to share their journey will quickly dismantle that pedestal. Be human with your students.

Do not blur the student-teacher relationship at any time. This type of relationship is sacred, and it is the teacher's responsibility to maintain the terms. The inherent power imbalance in this relationship will always blur the line between attraction and respect, distorting intentions and signals. We are required to act with ethical principles all the time, every time.

Teaching Yoga: Exploring the Teacher-Student Relationship by Donna Farhi is considered the most comprehensive book on the topic. She shares the knowledge she has gained from decades of practice and teaching, exploring with depth and compassion a variety of practical and philosophical topics such as:

- The student-teacher relationship and how to create healthy boundaries.
- How to develop physical and emotional safety for the students.
- Reasonable class sizes and how much they should cost.
- How to conduct the business of teaching while upholding the integrity of Yoga as a philosophy, a science, and an art.

I highly recommend any yoga teacher to read this book.

How to Get Your First Students

No one will show up to your classes if you do not market your offerings. An easy way to start getting your first students is by telling your friends and family you are finishing yoga teacher training and gaining experience as a teacher. I landed two jobs, one at a studio in the Netherlands and one in Vietnam, because my friends sent me job advertisements, and they knew I was looking for a teaching position.

Use your social media to put a message out there and let people know about your first class. Of course, there is also the old-fashioned way of picking up your phone to call friends and family. It still works.

Part of starting to teach yoga is to be a visionary and use your resources. Be proactive. Let people know that you are taking or have completed yoga teacher training; do not worry about the class size. We have all waited for students who never showed up, and we have all had classes where only one student came. Those are magical opportunities to grow as a teacher. So keep showing up and holding space, even if there are no students to fill it.

Eventually, students will come. In the meantime, stay focused on your teaching and remind yourself why you want to teach. If you are not teaching, you can't grow your skills. So start wherever you can, and watch your path unfold.

Getting Your First Experiences

When you are in the middle or have just completed teacher training, you can begin thinking about places where you will put your new skills to the service of others. During your training, you were immersed in a supportive and lively atmosphere. Unfortunately, that environment dissolves once you graduate, and you can feel lonely and puzzled about your next step. Figuring out how to start teaching can be daunting. While brainstorming ideas, I urge you to think "non-traditionally." If you research beyond yoga studios and health clubs, there are several other spaces to look into.

Yoga studios

To start teaching for your local yoga studio has its perks when you are a newbie. A studio provides you with a family of like-minded people and the opportunity to grow. Also, having more experienced teachers around will be very beneficial for your growth. Yoga studios will often challenge your comfort zone and invite you to expand your repertoire in terms of class offerings. I was scared when the studio asked me to start teaching a power yoga class, but thanks to the immeasurable support of the lead teacher, I gradually learned to feel comfortable with the speed and enjoy it.

Yoga studios often work based on seniority, and if you are the latest addition to the team, you might end up with only one class and at a not prime time of the day. Do not despair and be patient.

Health clubs and spas

Teaching yoga at a gym has pros and cons. Often you are the only "expert" around and left with a lot of freedom to teach in whatever shape or format you want. However, this means that you will have no one supporting your growth as a yoga teacher through exchange and feedback.

There is a myth that yoga in gyms is of low quality. I have only attended classes held in a health club while I was living in London in 2011, and all the teachers were very competent and knowledgeable. I learned a great deal from them. Nevertheless, the room was not ideal and often very noisy, particularly during Shavasana when people upstairs were bouncing on treadmills.

To conclude, I think that gyms are an alternative. However, we often will need to compromise with our ideal places and time to teach yoga if we want to make a living out of it.

Yoga studios and health spas are the only places listed here where you will not have to make an effort to attract students, as the company will market classes for you. However, the following suggestions are less conventional, so you will have to organize the class, promote it, and make sure everyone knows what to expect from it. We will talk about marketing more extensively in part three.

Outdoor locations

If you are lucky enough to live in a place with warmer weather and shorter winters, you have a longer season in which you can take advantage of free outdoor space. Scout for parks off the beaten path nearby and check their regulations for organizing activities. Alternatively, ask a friend if you can use their backyard. All you need is enough green space to lay out mats. I began my yoga career outdoors, leading Acro yoga groups in a park in the city of Breda. Sometimes it would start pouring rain and we had to run to find refuge in the train station nearby, where we would resume practicing under the curious eyes of the passengers.

Office buildings

I do not necessarily mean corporate businesses for office buildings, although those are an option, too. Scout the popular businesses downtown: coffee places, small boutiques, indoor markets, and see what their offerings are. When I moved to the U.S., I regularly attended a yoga class organized by an outdoor apparel shop. The teacher, who was also the store manager, held the class one hour before the shop would open to the public. It was a top-rated class, and I often ended up with my feet on top of the counter.

Dance or martial arts studios regularly have off-hours when the space is not used. You will discover that owners are always happy to collaborate and bring others into their space.

Religious institutions

Churches often offer their spaces free of charge to other organizations that fit their mission. Any of those spaces might work for teaching yoga classes. Talk with the facilities manager to find out if there is an interest.

Schools

There are two ways to approach schools: one way to get started is to teach yoga to school teachers. Second, to teach kids.

Use your connections to get in touch with someone from within the institution and find out if there are opportunities on the adult front.

For those interested in teaching kids, school districts have strict guidelines, and you are often required to have more than just a yoga certification. You can check for Montessori schools or home schools. They are always looking for additional activities to expose their kids to. Also, check for preschool or homeschool Facebook groups.

Local Centers

Community Centers

Most cities and towns have community centers. Besides the traditional recreational programs at the centers, many are looking to include new activities. Maybe yoga is not on their radar yet, but you can always propose it.

Senior centers and nursing homes

Senior centers and assisted living situations are always on the hunt for people willing to come in and teach classes. Seniors are increasingly interested in traditional as well as "gentle" or "chair yoga" classes. Get in touch with the people who are in charge of the location and make your pitch.

Nonprofit organizations

Nonprofits, like senior centers or Montessori schools, are always looking for volunteers. So if you are looking at a nonprofit, you might have to volunteer your time, but it is a great way to build your experience while giving back to your community.

Other Ideas

A spare room

I once fit fifteen ladies in a tiny living room to practice yoga. You do not need a dedicated room to teach. I still use my living room, though now only for online classes. Another example is that I used to attend Iyengar yoga classes in the spare room of a teacher's house—she only allowed six students per class. Tell your housemates that you want to teach your first classes in the comfort of your house. Make space for your growth.

Online teaching

One thing that yoga teachers have learned during this pandemic is that teaching online is an option. Current circumstances pushed us to get out of our comfort zone and turn into audio and visual magicians. Although online classes will never replace the experience of being in the presence and learning directly from a teacher, the pandemic has forced us to be creative in the way we approach yoga. Teaching online is a very low commitment. You can plan a class on zoom and share the link with your friends. However, it is a very different experience for the teacher as well, and it takes a while to learn how to juggle technology and students at the same time, so start small and eventually, more will come.

Hobbyists

If you have a hobby, you can try to connect it with yoga. For example, I often taught at my local climbing gym or spontaneously at the campsite after a long day of climbing. You will most probably be met with resounding affirmation by your peers. It doesn't need to be sport-related; whatever hobby you have—a book club or painting—you have a social group, and they might be interested in being exposed to yoga.

There are so many places available for you to teach. It often comes down to having the proper connection from within to make it happen. Before approaching any site, check in your network if someone knows someone. Personal relationships are always valuable. Otherwise, do Google and LinkedIn research to find out about the people. It is all about the people. Start attending their local events first, or buzz around the shop before approaching them. If the person in charge is never around, invite them to take some time to meet you. Once more, make space for your growth.

Yoga Elevator Pitch

I always go to a meeting prepared, or at least with a draft of a proposal. Make sure to have your yoga elevator pitch ready, which should highlight: who you are, your values, what you envision, and why you think this location would be a great fit. Additionally, bringing in successful stories will endorse your idea. Research examples of similar situations where a yoga class turned out to be a success!

Part III – Being a Teacher

This chapter will help you figure out your next steps after getting certified and give you tips on starting an exciting career in yoga. It is tough to begin full-time as a yoga instructor. I worked a classical 9-to-5 office job while teaching in the evening for about six months before deciding to make the switch. I lived almost in poverty for the following three years, and I only recently found financial stability.

Some people never make "the switch" and keep their full-time job all their life. I strongly advise you to hold on to it initially and slowly start transitioning, adding more classes to your schedule with time. As we will discuss more in-depth in the relationship with money, you cannot teach full-time or you will end up burnt out. The same applies to teaching and working a full-time job. You cannot teach more than two to four classes per week due to a lack of time and energy.

I wish I had someone advising me what things were critical after teacher training to start teaching, telling me how to get my first students, that I was worthy, and I should not be scared to charge for my classes. These important things are the topics of the following chapters.

To-do List for Yoga Yeachers

Start a certification folder

When you are tidy and organized, life flows better. Start fresh and collect all your certificates in one place and digitize them. I store them in an encrypted folder in the cloud.

You should also start a record with all classes you teach, the style, and the number of students attending—a simple spreadsheet will do the work. You will find it handy to have all the information in one place when applying for teaching positions.

Create a yoga resume or brochure

Stand out from the crowd with a well-designed resume that highlights your experience in the field.

Include all relevant experience, such as past teaching jobs (even in unrelated fields), how long you have practiced yoga, who your teacher is/was, and all the certificates you've collected. On my resume, I also added a mission statement which includes a few words on why I teach yoga and a description of my classes.

Get certified in CPR and EFAC

Show that you have taken a step further to becoming a professional member of the yoga community by getting certified in CPR (cardiopulmonary resuscitation for North American teachers) and EFAC (European First Aid Certificate for European teachers). It's unnecessary to take this step, but it comes with the bonus of professionalism. Be sure to add this certification to your folder and resume.

Liability insurance

Getting liability insurance is not mandatory for yoga teachers. Before even thinking about purchasing a policy, check what type of insurance your studio has and whether teachers fall in their plans. All the studios I have worked for never asked me to have my liability insurance, but some studios may require it as a condition of hiring you.

However, if you teach private classes at home or elsewhere, there are many insurance companies in the United States and Europe for your peace of mind. The basic yoga liability insurance protects yoga teachers, whether it's a student's medical bills, equipment loss, or a negligence lawsuit. Professional yoga insurance policies fall somewhere between $155 and $405 per year.

Gain classroom experience

As a recent yoga teacher graduate, you need to teach to stay active, gain experience, network, and keep learning by observing experienced teachers.

I am very much against free yoga, and I will tell you my reasons later on in the chapter. However, teaching free or donation-based classes is a great way to network and give back to the community. If you are new and need a jump-start, consider starting a yoga course at your local NGO or community center.

> *"The best way to find yourself is to lose yourself in the service of others."*
> — Mahatma Gandhi

Networking

To network is to connect with people who inspire you and support your growth. I would not be who I am without the care of my sangha, a Buddhist term that can be loosely translated as tribe, or community. Whether you are a new teacher or an expert, teaching yoga, like life in general, is not a solo performance. It is about finding the right people and building fond relationships. My "network" consists of yoga colleagues who were mentors and have become dear friends, students who attend my various yoga offerings, and of course, my precious family. Building a solid network is imperative to one's success in anything you do.

Networks are not built overnight. It requires time, effort, trust, and a willingness to pay it forward and share the love. Networks can be well-established forums for skill-shares, a group of teachers in your area to find substitutes for your classes, and support for your next big idea. And now, with social media, you can expand that network in ways that create endless potential. If you were to retain one thing from this chapter, remember to keep a contact list.

Marketing Tools for Yoga Teachers

Before marketing yourself, you need to decipher your niche: the style or type of yoga you will be teaching. It will support everything you do as a yoga instructor, from teaching to developing your website, and in the future, organizing workshops and running retreats.

Identifying your niche will also help you understand your target audience—your students. When you have a clear and focused niche, your marketing efforts will be much more impactful. For example, if your expertise is prenatal yoga, your market will be quite different from students who seek power classes. It takes time for teachers to identify their niche, so no worries if you still do not have one. When you are specialized in one field, it becomes easier to stand out in an already oversaturated teaching landscape. You will also feel more fulfilled teaching something that resonates with you. When you are authentic and not pretending to reach everyone seeking to practice yoga, your marketing efforts will attract authenticity, students will stick, and you will be successful. Do not neglect personal branding, and do not sell yourself short.

Let's now talk about marketing opportunities for yoga teachers.

Website

Once you have found your niche, something to consider is creating a website or a blog dedicated to your yoga journey. A website can help you display your "why," your teaching style, and your vision. It is the foundation for your marketing efforts. It will give you space outside class to show up for your audience and create a community. Many sites offer web hosting at reasonable rates. If you have never built a website before and do not know where to begin, consider bartering with a developer—you teach yoga to a designer who, in return, will develop your site. When applying for a job, make sure to mention your website and include the link in your resume.

In traditional digital marketing, a website is a hub where most people will interact with your business. All of your marketing efforts on other platforms will most likely send people to your website, whether to get information about your services and products, make bookings or purchases, or get contact details.

I dare to say that a yoga teacher doesn't need to have a website. A studio certainly does, but if you tend to be a contractor, you work for others. At the beginning of your career, you should focus your energy on building your resume or digital portfolio. On the other hand, a website is helpful if, for example, you teach in multiple locations, do private classes, or you run an online course. That is why you would have a professional-looking website that gives you credibility and allows you to take bookings and payments.

Social media

Before choosing which social media to focus on, it is worth investing time researching where your audience is active and which social platform they use. If your niche is yoga for climbers and your average student is a 30-year-old man that climbs, he won't likely use Pinterest. However, if your audience is moms, Pinterest could certainly be your go-to social media strategy.

Instagram

Nowadays, many yoga teachers use social media to make a name for themselves. Instagram is a great tool to keep students up to date on classes and share about the teacher's personal life and growth.

An Instagram feed, when done right, can be another way for us to show up for our students. There are plenty of resources out there to tell you how to become an Instagram guru. My only piece of advice to you is to stay humble, authentic, and don't let social media intoxicate you. A lot of people confuse the number of followers with how successful and skilled someone is. Your worth is not measured by social media success.

Tips for a successful Instagram page:
- **Build a business profile.** This capability gives you insights into followers and posts, promoting popular posts to reach more people.
- **Post often and be consistent.** Create a monthly schedule and post 2–3 times per week. My suggestion is to develop and plan posts a couple of weeks in advance. There is one rule about posting: be authentic. Don't show only your pretty poses, but use the platform to spread your message and reach your niche. Keep it honest and fun.
- **Try Instagram Stories.** Stories allow you to share multiple moments from your day in a combination of still images and short video clips. When you get the groove of it, Stories are entertaining! They disappear after 24 hours.
- **Post the link to your website in your bio.** You can always change this link to other lead magnets.

Pinterest

Pinterest is often a neglected social media tool for businesses, though it can increase traffic to your site, and it is relatively easy to use. Not everyone uses this social media, so make sure that your niche uses it before investing energies into it:

Tips for using Pinterest:
- **Set up your business account.** Like for Instagram, business accounts give you good insights and access to analytics.
- **Post often** and add at least 20 pins to each of your boards. Repost other pinned content too.
- **Image size is essential.** Use the Canva tool to create images of the correct size.
- Be sure to use WordPress Plugin that makes the images on your website "pin-able."

Facebook

With 1.7 billion users worldwide, leveraging Facebook to build your reputation and increase followers can bring you many new students. Not many teachers are making the most of their Facebook pages. Inviting all your friends to like your page can only get you so far; the same goes for sharing pretty pictures of yourself doing different yoga poses. Do not focus on having more followers. Focus on engaged followers who might become devoted students.

Begin by engaging your current followers. The Facebook algorithm will support you along the way by showing your content to their friends who are likely to engage with it. It takes time and effort, but if you are committed to making this happen, here are tips for maintaining an active presence on your Facebook page:
- **Create a business page** that is separate from your personal page.
- **Add a "call-to-action" button.** This button will direct people to your website or email newsletter sign-up page.
- After you run out of people in your network to "like" your page, you can invest in Facebook ads and target your exact

demographic. For example, if you teach yoga for runners, you can target people who run and are interested in healthy food.

- Post regularly.
- Post engaging content that calls for action. In other words, make posts that invite people to comment, like, or click a link.
- **Join other FB groups.** They offer great opportunities to connect with other like-minded people who could be your potential clients or readers one day.

YouTube

YouTube is another social media often used by yoga teachers. It is not easy to become a successful YouTuber nowadays, as it is a somewhat saturated market. Despite that, it is still worth creating a YouTube channel. It is a way to find new students and practice your teaching skills. Even though teaching to a camera does not substitute classroom experience, you can still learn transferable skills like crafting a flow and time management. Furthermore, when you apply for a teaching position at a yoga studio, the manager often asks for a class recording, and you can send the link to your YouTube channel.

You do not need to be tech-savvy or a professional movie editor. All you need to do is record yourself with a camera, get a few basic video editing skills under your belt, and upload videos to your YouTube channel.

Tips for starting a YouTube channel:
- **Match your vision to your channel.** As we have talked about before, make sure to know your niche.
- **Talk the language of your audience.** If you are teaching yoga for climbers, your videos should speak to them.

- **Be consistent with your content.** YouTube's algorithm recommends videos based on content. Making videos is about what interests you, but also what your audience expects from your content. It is your content that will keep them coming back for more. For example, suppose your channel is about yoga for climbers, and at one point, you start talking about kayaking. In that case, everyone will get confused: your viewers and YouTube's algorithm because they don't know what to expect from your content anymore.

- **Be consistent with your schedule.** Everyone loves consistency, including YouTube's algorithm and your followers. Make a realistic schedule: it takes time to film, edit, and upload content. You can schedule uploads so you always post at the right time, for instance, every Monday at 3:00 p.m. or every other Monday. There are no rules for how many videos you should post. Even once a month is enough.

- **Create a visual brand on YouTube.** You will likely want your thumbnails to have the same style over time so that your audience can quickly and easily find you and recognize you out of all the recommendations. It is also easy to organize content based on a particular theme or playlists: yoga for the evening and yoga to ease menstrual cramps. Your brand will unfold over time, and the visuals are things you can always change later. But thinking about your style will allow people to find you easily.

- **Research how to rank on the YouTube search engine.** Even with your brand and niche mapped out for you, it's worth researching trending topics and long-tail keywords that are relevant to your audience.

- **Film and edit your content.** The video quality matters, as does the editing. So before making your videos public for everyone to see, take the time to learn a few basic editing skills. Luckily for us, there are numerous tools out there that are very user-friendly and easy to understand.

LinkedIn is not the first social media that comes to mind when we think about yoga teachers. But it turns out to be very beneficial to those who know how to use it. For example, many yoga studio owners search for teachers on LinkedIn nowadays. So if you are looking to teach corporate yoga or get into private classes or own a studio, LinkedIn is a must-have social media platform to approach companies professionally.

I have landed several jobs on LinkedIn thanks to my personalized profile as a yoga teacher and digital marketing specialist. The LinkedIn profile page is the foundation for personal branding.

Here are few profile features you should focus on when building your profile on LinkedIn:

- **Choose the right profile picture.** It is your calling card on LinkedIn. In a nutshell, you want your profile picture to be a recent photo of your face in high resolution. Do not use an image of a yoga pose that might be a good fit for other social media. Pick a picture that shows your smiling face.
- **Add a background photo** that grabs people's attention, sets the context, and reveals more about your interest in yoga.
- **Make your headline attractive.** No rule says the description at the top of your profile page has to be just a job title. Use this space to communicate a bit more about your professional side.
- **Turn your summary into your story.** Your summary is your chance to tell your own story—so don't just use it to list your skills or the job titles you've had. Bring to life why those skills matter.
- **Expand your network.** Sync your profile with your email address book to grow your network quickly. This enables LinkedIn to suggest people to connect with.

- **Spotlight the services you offer.** This new LinkedIn feature was created for professionals who wear multiple hats. It helps contractors and freelancers showcase the range of services they offer. List what yoga services you can provide.
- **Spread the endorsement love.** Don't be afraid to reach out to people that you value or with who you've had a positive working experience for an endorsement. It's a common practice in the network.
- **Request recommendations.** Recommendations are personal testimonials written to illustrate the experience of working with you. Ask studio owners, other teachers, or students to write you recommendations.
- **Publications.** Use this feature to draw attention to the content you've created. Reading what other people have written gives us an idea if they would be a good fit for us.
- **Follow relevant influencers for your industry.** It helps to put a range of exciting content in your feed.
- **Publish long-form content—and use it to start conversations.** The more you share and comment on content, the more you establish your expertise and thought-leadership credentials on LinkedIn. Publishing long-form posts is a natural next step to take. A great starting point is to monitor the response that you get to your comments and shares.

Create an email and a professional signature

Having a dedicated yoga-related email will help you stay organized and look more professional in the eyes of potential employers.

One little trick I have learned is that signatures matter. Multiple people have read my blog and visited my digital marketing portfolio through my signature. Each email service provider has its own way of building a signature. Here are a few general guidelines:

- **Your name and surname should be on the first line.**
- **Include your job title**—for example, Yoga Teacher, Digital Marketing Specialist.
- **Add your contact information.** Your email, your phone number, and your location if you wish.
- **Incorporate the primary social media:** LinkedIn, Instagram, Facebook page. Include only the relevant ones. If you don't have a Facebook page, or if it's inactive, don't add it.
- **Hyperlink your website and portfolio.**
- **Add your logo** (optional).

Andrea Martina Zaghi-Ganter

Yoga teacher | Digital Marketing Strategist

Albuquerque, USA: +1 xxxxxxx
Bologna, Italy: +39 xxxxx xxxxx
Linkedin | Instagram | Portfolio|
xxxxxxxxxxxxxxxxxx@gmail.com

Flyer and business card

A more traditional but still effective way to put yourself out there and attract new students is to create flyers and business cards with your offerings. You can drop them off in the waiting rooms of bodyworkers, chiropractors, and other complementary medicine practitioners. Do not forget the bulletin board of your favorite coffee place.

Conclusions

In a book about the art and business of teaching yoga, I must talk about marketing, but you do not have to do any of that. Ultimately, being a good teacher and word-of-mouth are still the best marketing tools.

Nevertheless, if you are willing to begin a marketing journey, those above are some options. My suggestion is to start from what you are familiar with and continue from there. Once again, know your audience and what (social) media they use before embarking on a digital marketing journey. If your specialty is chair yoga, your best bet is to drop flyers where people can see them, as that typical client may not use social media.

If you think that marketing is crucial for you, but you cannot be bothered with it, one option is to hire an expert or a freelancer to support you and take some weight off your shoulders.

Allow yourself to grow and develop as a teacher. Building a career as an independent contractor takes time. If you find yourself distressed or frustrated, call on the yogic action of *tapas—discipline—* and persevere through the difficult moments with the knowledge that you have chosen a path that offers enormous benefits to yourself and others.

Give and Receive

Talking about money and worth is never an easy topic for yoga teachers. Most of us are not on this path to becoming rich but rather finding a more fulfilling life. However, as you paid money to become a certified yoga instructor and keep investing in your education, it is appropriate to expect students to pay you in exchange for your services. If we were to give without receiving constantly, we would quickly feel depleted, burnt out, and under-appreciated.

Money is a form of energy. We most frequently use it in exchange for goods and services, but we can agree to accept any currency we value. We would then call it bartering.

When we do not have to pay for a service, we don't consider them as binding. Students are more likely to commit to your classes when they have paid for them in one way or another. Would you question an airline that charged you to take a flight? So why do we struggle to think of a yoga class in the same way? We want students to commit to their practice and experience the transformation that only consistency on the mat can give them.

If you are not charging for your classes, you communicate that you do not value what you offer.

Keep in mind that you are being kind and giving back to your community by teaching yoga and sharing your wisdom with others, even when you do receive something in return. When you feel called to share more, offer a free or donation-based class every week or volunteer to teach at homeless shelters, assisted living homes, and community centers. For everything else, gratefully accept payment as a token of a student's appreciation for what you do. You deserve it.

Paying the Bills As a Yoga Teacher

According to ZipRecruiter, which makes salary estimates based on employer job postings and third-party data sources, a yoga teacher in the United States makes a yearly average of $45,000. In 2015, CNN ranked Pilates and yoga teaching as one of the best 100 jobs in America, with a median annual salary clocking in at $62,400.

The truth is that this is not true for most yoga teachers. To reach that figure, you would have to teach twenty-six yoga classes per week for a whole year, at the rate of $50 per class. First of all, this hourly rate is not commonplace for most studios. Second, if you teach five classes per day, Monday to Friday, trust me, you would get burnout. In my best months, I earn roughly $1,300 a month by teaching seven hours per week in two different studios, one physical and one online.

There are two options to make a sustainable living as a yoga teacher, excluding teaching twenty-six classes per week at a studio, which is not sustainable: the first one is to have someone else paying the bills. The second is to diversify your income outside the studio.
We will discuss the second approach.

Diversify Your Income

The income of yoga teachers ranges tremendously; while most teachers earn less than $30k per year, some teachers earn $300,000 or more.

The teachers who earn the most all have one thing in common: they have multiple income streams. In other words, they get paid from some combination of workshops, training, online sponsorships, and more.

There are two distinct ways to diversify your income: you can stay in the wellness field by becoming a massage therapist or life coach. The other option is to diverge entirely from this field and learn a different skill, like coding or digital marketing.

Personally, after being a yoga teacher and a masseuse simultaneously, I realized that this combination was not working for me. I needed to do something outside the holistic realm where I could tap into different energies. So, after some trial and error, I chose digital marketing as an opportunity to diversify my income, and I use my extensive knowledge of yoga to stand out from the crowd. I still spend my days thinking and learning about yoga, just in different forms.

I broke down different income opportunities into two buckets:

- Beginner-friendly income opportunities

- Intermediate and advanced income opportunities

Diving into your skills repertoire is the best way to find the most effective ways to diversify your yoga teacher income. Look at those things that give meaning to your life, your passions, and see if you can turn them into commodities. You can always learn new skills, too. I was not "trained" as a writer, but I always had a great passion for reading. So, here I am, getting paid to write about yoga. As always, take what works and leave the rest. It is not an easy process to acquire a new skill. You will have to invest time and money. You will not just read through the following list and pick a random one but you could get inspired. It's best to start thinking about outside studio hours as soon as possible.

Beginner-Friendly Income Opportunities

Beginner-friendly income opportunities are low risk and low investment, and you can get started right away. They are ideal for new teachers and those who are just getting started diversifying their income.

Teach classes at nearby colleges

Some universities will hire yoga teachers to offer classes to their students. Try contacting the "Student Services" or "Rec Center" to inquire about job opportunities. They often pay more than studios.

Corporate group yoga classes

Corporate yoga classes are a great way to improve workplace morale, increase productivity, and bring employees together to do something fun. It is becoming quite popular for organizations to provide free yoga classes to their employees as part of their benefits—most successful teachers in this space charge a flat rate between $70 to $200 per class.

Ask your local network and do some Google research to find out which company would be a viable candidate in your area.

Freelance writer for yoga publications

If you like writing, this can be a great way to make extra money while networking with the yoga industry. The perks of this opportunity are that you get to read and learn so much about yoga.

Offer private yoga lessons

Private lessons are a way to increase your income while helping your students grow in their practice. Private lesson prices typically range from $50 to $200 per hour. You could also offer private classes via Zoom.

Podcasting about yoga

If you have a passion for conversations and have a lot to say, podcasting can be your go-to activity. It is similar to the concept of blogging in terms that you can build an audience, but it takes a long time to earn money with it. Luckily, it's easy to get started: you need a microphone and exciting themes to discuss. Besides building traffic to your website, if you have one, once you gain popularity, you can start earning money by selling sponsored ads at the beginning of your episodes.

Digital marketing

You could make a good living by teaching yoga and freelancing as a digital marketing specialist as a side hustle. Valuable skills in this realm include Website development and UX and UI design, email marketing, social media, SEO knowledge, paid advertisements, and previous experience as an event organizer.

I started freelancing back in 2017 when I began my adventures around the world. At first, I accepted everything that came to me: I translated documents from Italian to English and vice versa, wrote blog posts, and managed IG accounts. I did not have a plan or a direction. Freelancing is a broad term. When the pandemic hit, I enrolled in a Digital Marketing Bootcamp. The course taught me the essentials skills to progress, give direction to my freelancing career, and start making real money. I learned the fundamentals of SEO and linked new knowledge to my passion for content and yoga, which became my niche.

Intermediate and Advanced Income Opportunities

Although the following opportunities have the potential to increase your income dramatically, they require business strategy and long-term planning. To successfully undertake one of these alternatives, you should already be an established teacher in your community and have a passion for entrepreneurship.

Create an online course

Consider turning your knowledge of yoga into an online course. There are endless opportunities in the yoga space: intro to yoga, how to launch a yoga retreat successfully, how to create a yoga sequence, etc. Create a course for students who want to learn and deepen their practice without necessarily wanting to teach.

Run a yoga retreat

I suggest planning your first retreat locally. It is less risky and potentially more profitable than an international one. There is always the option to partner up with another yoga teacher. There is also the option to create a hybrid yoga retreat, combining yoga with another discipline. For example, Jennifer Pastiloff combines yoga with writing. My friend Vera organizes retreats blending yoga with climbing. They are both very successful.

Create a workshop

Develop a unique 2- to 3-hour workshop to deliver at yoga studios. Consider your expertise and what yoga students are looking to learn about. If you like traveling, consider pitching your workshop to studios while on the road.

Become the manager at your local studio

If you are organized and have people skills, consider applying as a studio manager. This opportunity allows you to increase your total income and have more regular hours, and you will also understand better the mechanisms behind the scene of owning a studio.

Get more certifications

As mentioned before, you can become a massage therapist or a health coach, nutrition coach, etc.

Mentor new yoga teachers

With over 15,000+ people becoming certified to teach yoga each year, the practice of having a mentor to help new teachers kick off their careers will be more and more required.

Conclusion

Making a decent living as a yoga teacher is challenging but not impossible. You might need to find a part-time job that you do not like initially while learning how to diversify your income outside the studio. Do not give up if you cannot find the right formula straight away, give yourself time, and don't settle if you are not happy. My advice is to reach out to people who seem to have figured it out and talk to them. They can give you the support you need.

Part IV – Interview with Yoga Teacher and Former Studio Owner Dorinda Farver

Dorinda was born and raised in Pennsylvania, U.S.A. She is a 500-hour certified teacher that has found both a challenge and an incredible peace in the magic of yoga. She has lived in the Netherlands since 1992 and discovered her fondness for this ancient wisdom in the late '90s.

Many others followed her first teacher training with Tonnie Goes. She trained with David Swenson, Shiva Rea, Neva Ingalls, Robert Boustany, and Gurmukh Kaur Khalsa.

In the autumn of 2020, she sold the studio that she founded, Yogasite. She wanted to focus more on her new coaching company, Sensei, while she continued to l teach at the studio, and she is still the building owner. In this interview, she unveils her experiences as a student, teacher, and studio owner.

The first time I attended Dorinda's classes, I felt intimidated by her energy. It's hard to describe, but she always pressed the right buttons and filled me with awe. During the 200-hour yoga teacher training with her and Robert Boustany, I tapped into a deeper wisdom and began experiencing yoga as a union of my body, mind, and spirit. As I was maturing as a teacher, also my relationship with Dorinda had changed. I found myself closer to her and her energy more approachable. I will never forget an analogy she gave during the teacher training: she made her hands into fists and started shaking one, keeping the other still. She said: "This one (showing the still hand) is you, grounded and stable. The other one represents your family and yoga students." Then, she brought the shaky hand closer to the still one, and it stopped shaking. Groundedness is an essential part of every yoga teacher.

Life had brought us in a different (physical) direction, but her openness and availability to share her story with me endorsed my affection and esteem for Dorinda. The essence of Yogasite is awareness, understanding, acceptance, harmony, and love. I genuinely wish for any inspiring yoga instructor to find a place such as this studio has been for me. This interview has been edited and approved by the interviewee.

Andrea Zaghi: Hello Dorinda! Thank you for taking the time today. Let's kick off this interview: where did the idea of opening Yogasite come from?

Dorinda Farver: I was thirty-six-years old when I took my first yoga class. It went pretty fast from there. I have a degree in Architecture and Design, and I used to work in the art and creative industries. In 2003 when I moved to Breda, my husband was working at a hospital, my kids were little, and I discovered yoga. I followed Nathalie, a British woman, all around Breda to take her classes. No one else taught it at that time, and everything was less professional. Yoga was taught in somebody's attic or living room, and at that time, it wasn't even offered at gyms.

After a year of taking classes from Nathalie, she moved back to England. Nathalie rented space from Lilian, who suggested to me that I take over the classes, saying, "I will pay for half of your teacher training if you keep running the classes and renting a space from me." Teaching was not in my plans, but I agreed anyway. I got my teacher training half-paid for and inherited four classes before I did anything. Thank you, universe! I felt called to teach yoga. After that happened, everything started unfolding, and I have never stopped growing. I kept renting from Lilian for two years. She rented her space out to other people as well and, at one point, did not have enough room and hours for me to expand anymore. So I found a new space to share with another teacher called Anne, who turned out to be a bit unstable. I stayed with her for only eight months before finding my own space. My classes started expanding, and I hired Laura, whom you know as well, to teach with me. At one point, Annelies showed up in my life, and everything took off.

The way our relationship started is funny: she was a dancer and used to work at De Stilte, a dance company. I was teaching yoga there when she decided to take a course with me. At the same time that her contract with the dance company was ending, my nanny program was ending too. She said, "I will do it. I will move in with you and help you out with the kids."

She ended up living with me for five years. And because she was there, I could start building the foundation of Yogasite. My husband was not around most of the time because of his job. Financially I was fine, but if it was not for Annelies, Yogasite would have probably never existed.

Andrea: How long did it pass before your call to open a yoga studio in Breda became a reality?

Dorinda: It took about five years until it kicked off, even though it was already legally a company. I rented a room in the building that I now own, which used to be a Community Center maintained by the town. At one point, they asked all the renters to leave because the building was going to be sold. At this stage, the studio was becoming successful, and I was looking to buy another building. I tried to buy four different spaces already, and none had worked out. Owning the building was also part of my vision: I wanted it to be spacious enough to have more renters that would help me to maintain it and turn it into a community.

Andrea: Had you ever been an entrepreneur before opening Yogasite?

Dorinda: I have had other experiences before owning my own company, so I consider myself an entrepreneur. But this was different, it was a calling, and I did not care what anybody told me. I was determined to do it, and Annelies helped me out. She had been dramatically affected in a positive way by meeting me and starting yoga. She believed in me and my idea, in what Yogasite was supposed to be like and represent for the community.

I was not in it for the money, and that is why it worked out. I still needed money to build it. But I honestly believe that without that inspiration, that energetic connection of that was what I was supposed to do, I would not have made it. I see yoga as managing magic. Sometimes, I did not know what was coming, and I needed to trust the process.

You cannot explain yoga in a standard way, like Robert's Pralaya yoga, he calls it non-linear. There is no actual "rule book" for it. He does not even know what he is going to do; he does what is needed at the moment. Often students ask me, "is he going to do a workout in the morning?" and I will ask him, and he will say "Yes," but then he won't, and he'll do something completely different. I believe that the yoga that we're doing at Yogasite is from a source that Yoga Alliance cannot check. I believe it's magical. I believe it's love. I believe it's energy. I believe it's healing. And I believe that this is also what gave me the vision to do this. I did not always make logical choices in the process; I mostly followed my guts and instinct. If someone tried to sell me something or manipulate me and it did not feel right in my heart, I would not do it. I did not want anyone trying to sell my students more s***! I wanted people to feel the studio was a home, a safe place to open up, be courageous and heal.

Andrea: How did you find yoga teachers for the studio?

Dorinda: Almost all of the teachers at Yogasite have done the teacher training with Robert and me. I hired two teachers who did not do the training with us, and it did not work out so well. Their energy did not fit with the students nor the studio.

It is a bureaucratic nightmare to hire people in the Netherlands, so the teachers are independent contractors.

Most teachers do not work full-time at one studio because it's exhausting to teach more than ten classes a week. As a teacher, it is difficult to do it, and as a studio owner, you cannot pay people more than is coming in, and that's also part of the problem of making a living as a yoga teacher. If there are only four people in the class paying €10 each, you cannot pay the teacher €40, because you also have to cover the rent of the space, the bills and everything behind the scenes. So I gave all the teachers a flat fee of €10, even if nobody showed up. On top of that, they made an additional €2.50 per attendee up to a maximum of €30.00 per class. This way, they had a motivation to fill up their classes so they could make more. However, when they organized their workshops, I gave them 60% of the income. I was encouraging them to develop their specialization within the community and, at the same time, earn more money.

Andrea: How did you help teachers with marketing?

Dorinda: I helped them mainly through the website and social media of Yogasite. We would think about the promotion of the workshops, and everyone would then register through Yogasite, so teachers didn't have to take payments or deal with phone calls and inquiries. At the end of it, we just gave them 60% of the total income that came in from the workshop. So that is not a bad deal because teachers have to focus on designing the workshop and teaching.

I know of successful teachers who opened their yoga studios and are having a hard time. It is not easy teaching and managing the studio at the same time. When people who can't get in the Zoom link, call you while you are about to start a class because there is no one else to pick up the phone, it can be very challenging and frustrating.

Andrea: If you want to focus on teaching and organize your classes outside a studio, do you need a manager?

Dorinda: That depends. As I said, I think either stay small or go big. In that middle phase, when you have to hire front desk personnel to manage bookings and take the phone calls, it is expensive, and if you are not well established, it is hard to get by.

If you are maintaining a community, you can't just walk away. You cannot travel a lot and maintain the community at the same time. It would help if you had someone you trust and that shares your vision, like Annelies was there for me at Yogasite.

The real deal for yogis or people who don't mind traveling, like David Swensen, is to organize workshops abroad. He always honors the yoga studios because he knows how hard it is to maintain the community. I remember him saying: *"I have the best deal here because I'm the fun uncle who shows up, and everybody is happy to see me. And then I leave!"*

But not everyone is David Swensen and gets invited everywhere either. That's a reputation, and it takes time to build it. I honestly believe that if teaching yoga is not your calling, it is really hard to make it.

Andrea: Or you keep it small?

Dorinda: Well, you can. Or it's a commercial business like a gym. Fine. I'm not criticizing that because that's where many people get their first taste of yoga. I think it is easier to maintain a gym than a yoga studio. But I have never owned a gym, so I do not know.

Andrea: How did you come about the business model of Yogasite?

Dorinda: I tried to think what was fair and financially possible for me. It was not easy at first. Annelise and I were too nice, and we talked to anybody who had a problem of any kind, and we would work out a solution. Which is a lovely approach, but it costs time and money. We also let students run up debt that they could pay out later, and we would find ourselves chasing them for money at the end of the month. Yoga should be accessible to everyone, but you cannot do it free of cost. A great idea I always wanted to implement but have not managed yet is to set up a grant program that allows people who can afford it to donate yoga classes to people who cannot afford it.

At the beginning of Yogasite, a lot of the workforce was involved in running the background. We did not used to have a sound accounting system, so every bill was done by hand. Now we finally switched to an online booking and payment system, and that goes much easier. But you cannot afford that system if you're not big enough. However, with the pandemic and the shift to remote classes, the number of systems available increased, and their price dropped. I wasn't born as tech-savvy. So I had to adapt to technology.

Andrea: Have you ever had to ask students or teachers to leave the studio?

Dorinda: I have had to confront people who just did not fit with the studio's energy. For example, I had a teacher who spoke very directly and offended students without realizing what she was doing.

I was talking about creating a safe space. And she thought that I meant safety. She told me she could cue poses correctly and made sure everyone was following the proper alignments.

I meant that students would feel energetically safe and at home and ok to let go emotionally or fall apart in the class. She didn't get it. We discussed it, and it wasn't a pleasant conversation because she did not understand what I was saying. We weren't on the same page.

Top teachers have an overage of 30 to 40 students per class and mostly returning ones. Some other teachers have only a few students. So what is it that they have that other teachers don't?

Andrea: It is not something that you can teach in a 200-hour training. It is something that comes with experience.

Dorinda: And that is the tricky part. When I am teaching, words come out of my mouth, and people melt. I don't even know why I'm saying it or what I'm saying half the time. When new students come to an introduction class with me and at the end of the class, they're sitting in the back of the classroom, in tears, asking themselves: "What has just happened to me?"

To me, creating a safe space means connecting students to their prana, to the energy, to love, to something that opens their hearts and souls. As a yoga teacher, I am trying to talk to my student's souls. It's not about the pose that I tell them to do. A pose is a tool that works because I can distract them by giving them detailed instructions and let them open up into some energy that is yoga. It requires time. I can't force people to go faster. I never know when the shift is going to happen or what it's going to look like. I let it go when it does.

Andrea: Did you ever have difficulties with students at Yogasite?

Dorinda: I have never had anyone injured. Some people do not like me for different reasons, that's why I want to have a variety of teachers. Some people do not come to my classes because I am fiery, and I push buttons. Not on purpose. It just happens. It can be confronting.

They might say, "I don't like her classes!" or "She talks too much." I do talk a lot in class. Sometimes I have stopped in the middle of a power yoga class and meditated. And everybody melted. Because that's what needed to happen. I don't follow the rules when I'm in that zone.

My students know it. They also know when somebody is giving them a cookie-cutter lesson. They don't want that anymore. That's part of the problem. Once you've come and you've experienced classes like this, you do not want the cookie-cutter anymore. You want your soul spoken to. And I think so many people are longing for that more than anything. As a teacher, you need to have the courage to find your authenticity. You need to be willing to take a risk, to lose, or win big.

I also believe that not everybody needs to like me; there are a lot of people who do and place trust in me. And I need to respect that trust. I've witnessed how some teachers take advantage of their students. I know I have the power, but understanding that power is not something that I want to abuse.

Andrea: How do you see the teacher-student relationship?

Dorinda: When students connect to the energy or open their hearts in yoga, they experience a love they have never felt before. Sometimes they mistakenly attribute that feeling of love with falling in love with their teachers. This affection can get to the ego of their teacher.

Robert says: "You (teacher) have to be ferocious; otherwise, your students will eat you." They want more of that love. You need to have pure intentions when you're teaching at that level because your students' safety comes first.

If the teacher is taking advantage of people, they lack self-love. It is challenging for yoga studios to control that because they trust the teacher in the first place. However, if a teacher wants to take advantage of their students, they have the power to do that.

When I'm in that energy, healing can take place. I see miracles. I watch them daily. Strangers whom I don't even know their names, but energetically I see what's going on with them. And they melt in front of me. I can walk out the door and never see them again. And their life may have shifted because something cleared up, they can finally see, and they're feeling lighter. Or the pain they were carrying around isn't there anymore. You do yoga to bring the karma to the surface and clear it. Once all your karma is gone, your soul doesn't have to come back.

I was reading a quote from Yogananda the other day that said: *"Persons who pass their lifetime satisfying the body and gratifying the ego, unaware of the Divine Image in themselves, amass earthly karma or sins. When they die with those unresolved karmic consequences and with unfulfilled earthly desires, they must reincarnate again and again to resolve all mortal entanglements."*

If you were a liar or a cheater before you died, you are going to be that when you come back. You are coming back with the same energy and the same bucket of s*** to work with as you did when you left. Living in this body, at this moment, is your opportunity to work through that. You can't run away from it; sooner or later, you will have to deal with it. Karmically, nothing can happen to you that's not supposed to happen. These things that are happening to people in yoga studios are karma. So that they can start clearing, standing up to something, and beginning to face their challenges. It might not always be a pleasant journey, as many painful and uncomfortable truths might come to the surface; it is the teacher's responsibility to create a safe space for them to freak out and feel grounded enough to handle it.

Andrea: Thank you! I'm so happy you are saying this. Every teacher needs a mentor, to learn how not to fall apart and to keep growing, and be the best of yourself when you show up.

Dorinda: I would love to set a platform where I can support yoga teachers and studios to stay energetically connected. Even when things are falling apart, how do you allow it to fall apart without freaking out, so there's room for you to grow again? I want to support the people who are helping other people. And I know from my own experience you cannot do that without an energetic connection. You cannot figure it out all in your head.

Andrea: Oh, how much I miss the community at Yogasite. I would like to know more about the role of teacher training programs for the studio's financial health. Can you start by telling me how you met Robert, the other lead teacher for the 200- and 500-hour programs?

Dorinda: Like I was called to teach yoga, I knew I would find a mentor, but I was aware that he was not in Holland. I couldn't go anywhere because my kids were little, so he needed to come to me. One day, I got a phone call from Diane, a woman from Texas, who's telling me that Robert is coming to Belgium and they're looking for a studio for him to teach at in the Netherlands. She found my name and telephone number on crazy Anna's website. I told you I worked with a crazy woman for a little bit, right? This is why I had to be at her studio. Because Diane found my name and phone number on Anna's website and she called me directly. It was a sign, and I was receptive to it. A month later, Robert showed up to teach a workshop. He was running late. But when he walked in and sat down, I knew Robert was my mentor. For the next few years, he came to my studio when he traveled overseas from Houston to teach workshops. Within a year, we decided that we would organize a 200-hour teacher training at Yogasite together.

I started wrong financially because I gave Robert everything that came in. That is not a good financial model for a studio. At first, he would come to teach, and I'd hand him an envelope full of money. There were no questions from him or me but total trust. He never demanded anything from me. We had not discussed wages; we just went with the flow.

Then I finally talked to him and agreed that he would take a percentage of what comes in. This type of deal is how it works when well-known yogis give a workshop at a hosting studio. There is a 60-40% split, and they take the higher percentage. Sometimes I had famous teachers from the U.S. over to the studio, and they asked for 70% and part of their travel costs paid for. So there's not much profit for the yoga school left if you're hiring someone to run the teacher training. So to make it profitable, I started to be part of the teacher training. For the 200-hour teacher training, students do half of it with Robert and half of it with me. Robert does not always teach the sun greetings and the basics in detail. He's at an advanced level. So I was doing the basics. Then Yogasite managed to make some profit.

If a yoga school develops its own teacher training and the owner is the lead teacher, the studio can profit. But if you need to pay the teacher, the bills, the accommodation, etc., it becomes hard to break even. So this year, when I sold Yogasite in October, it was the first time I got paid personally for what I am doing and made a small monthly salary. Everything else I did always went back to Yogasite.

Andrea: Was it financially worth it to own a yoga studio? Did you manage to make a profit, or were you always on the edge of breaking even?

Dorinda: I always paid my bills on time, and we even made a small profit. But every time you grow, you have to invest more. And so I bought the building, invested in new systems, and invited teachers over, which all costs money. I was the owner; therefore, I was the cash cow. If something broke or needed to be replaced, people gave the bill to me.

Andrea: What advice would you give me if I tell you that I want to open my own yoga studio?

Dorinda: What are your goals? Do you want freedom? Do you want independence? From my experience, you can make more money staying small and just getting paid for what you do than hiring other people. So you either stay small or get big. But there's a lot of growing pains in the middle of it.

Andrea: It's hard because when you're small, you need to do everything yourself: finance, marketing, PR, etc., sometimes it is too much, and I feel my enthusiasm to teach yoga fading.

Dorinda: Exactly. Annelies worked with me and should have gotten paid ten times more for the hours she did. She sacrificed herself and so did I for Yogasite. But we wanted it, and we believed in it, and that's what we felt called to do. So, should you open your yoga studio? If this is not your calling, it might be challenging. You have to be supported by some angels up there who save you when things are going down. I got saved again and again and again when I thought it was over.

Corona and the restrictions are killing the business now. People are so fed up with doing everything online. I am not sure what's going to happen in the future. I sold the studio last fall, but I still teach there, and I want to see it thrive. Community connection is needed more than ever.

Andrea: The community is a reason worth fighting for.

Dorinda: It has to be. If you're looking to get paid for every hour you are working, you won't make it. It would not have worked without Annelies; I did not want to do the marketing or the finance. I would have quit long ago if she didn't take over the administration. I don't care how much money comes in. And that's why I'm a terrible businessperson with a successful company. But to make it work, you need someone doing the paperwork behind the scene. People know I'm not just trying to take their money. They know I care. And this is what makes it thriving.

There was a point when my kids were little that I did not want to do it anymore. The studio was getting too big, too busy, and I couldn't deal with all of these other things altogether. So I was ready to quit when Annelies stepped in. I wouldn't have done this without her. She believed in what I was doing. She was put on my path, and I was put on her path. And we built it together, even though my name is on it. I am the energy in the front, but she did all of the details in the back. I do not think anyone else would have done what she did for Yogasite.

Andrea: How has your relationship with money changed since you began teaching yoga?

Dorinda: When I first started, I did not have the talents I have now. I feel comfortable charging more because what I offer is worth more. Word-of-mouth is the most valuable marketing tool because it builds a genuine and confirmed reputation. By doing the right thing over and over and over again, you create real value. Marketing it more does not make it more valuable.

Andrea: What is your opinion on making a full-time living by teaching yoga?

Dorinda: I think yogis need an alternative income. Very few people manage to make a full-time living by only teaching yoga without turning it into a marketing show; it's not easy. But, I don't want to judge anyone for where they are on their path. When you are ready for something more meaningful, your heart will call. Enjoy your life!

Andrea: Understanding that being a yoga teacher is something that you can only do part-time but demands a lifelong investment is not well addressed in the yoga community. It is hard to find an alternative income that contributes to your financial stability but at the same time fulfills your soul. Teacher training programs do not talk about this because the lead teachers are making a living out of yoga most of the time.

Dorinda: Yoga teacher training should be about you developing yourself and sorting stuff out. It should be for your growth and not necessarily only to teach yoga. You may end up doing it afterward, but the reason to enroll in teacher training is to deepen your yoga practice. People make significant shifts when they go through teacher training. Past traumas and karma come to the surface when we do energetic work. And that is why you're going through yoga teacher training, dealing with your issues first so that you can stand in front of a group of people, be open energetically, and handle whatever is going on in the class. For example, if I am not clean energetically, I can't deal with somebody falling apart in class. Making somebody cry is not your goal; your goal is to create a safe space for them to do it.

Andrea: Why did you decide to sell Yogasite?

Dorinda: Deciding to sell the studio and committing to it has been a several years' process. When Annelies started her family and began to work fewer hours, things shifted. I hired someone to help with the administration, and the teachers and staff were all moving and changing. This past year has been a roller coaster. I'm in the front, and everybody behind was asking, "Where's this roller coaster going?" and I replied: "I don't know!" It was getting dangerous, and people kept asking: "Where are we going with this?" And I said, "I still don't know, but I'm not leaving." Some people jumped off the roller coaster. Some people stayed on board. I seriously didn't know where the roller coaster was going. And everybody was mad at me because I didn't know where it was going. But I never jumped off the ride.

I didn't think that I wanted to sell it. It was rough for a while; people began leaving and being very upset with how things were going. It was not flowing well below the surface. But we kept trying, we switched booking systems and did some other stuff, and then Corona hit.

The contracts of several employees ended last June. At one point, one of my old teachers, Ellen, who was living in Valencia with her husband at that time, reached out to me. For them, Yogasite was like a family, and they were interested in buying it. I kept thinking that I had to maintain all of this together because I was the founder. At Robert's teacher training last spring, I had a meltdown during which I finally accepted and realized that I did not have to take care of all of this by myself.

We went back and forth for several months before agreeing on a price. What is the value of Yogasite? To me, it's priceless. I negotiated a deal with them that included all of the studio's props, the client list, the logo, and the name. Selling Yogasite was a painful process. It felt like I was letting them adopt one of my children: "I want you to take care of it." The studio was precious to me, what I represented, and stood for.

Annelies is the one who made the deal happen. She was the glue between us when our egos were clashing. She still works with me, and she's managing the building now. So although they're now the official owners, I'm still there as a teacher, a face and owner of the building.

I'm slowly moving away from group yoga classes. I have recently become an ICF certified coach, and I'm heading toward corporate coaching and training.

Andrea: What do you think of the role of the Yoga Alliance as an institution trying to regulate teacher training?

Dorinda: I understand why they're doing it, but I also think it's ridiculous at the same time. Who are they to say that I'm a good teacher or not? They've never seen me teach. They didn't give me a certificate, but they assume I am a good teacher because I pay a yearly fee.

Some of the top teachers in the world are not registered with Yoga Alliance, but they know more than anybody about yoga. I understand why they do what they do. Nowadays somebody can take a weekend course and say that they're a yoga teacher. They legally can do that.

And so, the Yoga Alliance wants to make sure certain things are covered during teacher training. Are they doing a good job? It is not my job to judge this.

Andrea: Many modern studios have turned down anything that recalls the spiritual and more traditional aspects of yoga. For example, by asking their teachers to use only English words and avoid chanting. The justification behind these choices is inclusivity: spiritual elements might turn down certain people,

therefore they are banned so that everyone can feel welcome. What's your opinion about this?

Dorinda: What makes it yoga is the energy. Sometimes, people who take a class with me will say, "Oh, it's not spiritual. We didn't chant. It's not..." But they're crying at the end of class.

The energy is necessary to make it yoga. And the energy is, if that's what people are calling it, spiritual. So I do not think every teacher is connected and channels energy, but that is yoga.

I do not know what I'm going to say half the time in class, but it's healing and magical. I believe that's what is calling students out here. Energy holds the power of transformation.

I have people saying to me: "I'm not going to your class. You freak me out!"

But I also have people who come to one of my classes, get freaked out but want to come back because finally, someone had authentically spoken to their soul. People don't get that very often. Maybe this is not the most popular route, but that's ok. I do what needs to be done at the moment. I can't dictate that from before. I have an idea of what I'm going to teach, have a topic in mind, and set boundaries for the class. But there is power in freedom. This is the way Robert teaches as well. If you need to know what will happen beforehand, you will have an exciting challenge when coming to us.

I remember one time I saw people heal energetically. I can't even explain this. This experience was more magical than anything I've ever witnessed. During lunchtime at a teacher training weekend, Robert was sitting on the couch, and there were people on either side of him in tears. I'm standing there talking to two of the other students. One of them said, "Why is everybody crying? Why is everybody melting? I don't know why everybody is behaving in this way, what's going on here? It's kind of weird." And I say, "Well, you know, sometimes energy moves!" Robert looks up at the woman standing with me, and points to her chest: "What is that?" And he does something with his hand. She burst out in tears just standing there. He can see energy. He can see when there's an energy blockage.

I know things sometimes, but I don't know how I know them. This knowledge doesn't come from a book. When I'm energetically connected to the moment, my intuition gives me information. Energy is full of information. The more I relate to that energy, the more data I have. When I am teaching a class, I have no judgment other than I have to be here in this love so people can tap into this energy and begin their healing process. Whether they shift or not is none of my business.

Andrea: I will never stop being a student, and our conversation is a reminder of how much I still want to learn. It is at your studio that I established a connection with my energy for the first time. I've changed and grown so much since then, but through all the experiences and places that I've been, I struggled to find a community like the one that I found at Yogasite. I had no idea what we had until I moved away, and I didn't.